D0538301

VINOBURGER

GOURMET BURGERS INSPIRED BY THE CUISINES
OF THE WORLD'S GREATEST WINE REGIONS

by

JEFF BRAMWELL

with

JAY MURRIE

photography by

JOYCE BRAMWELL

PUBLISHED BY FREE RUN CREATIONS LLC

Copyright ©2010 by Jeff Bramwell
All photography ©2010 by Joyce Bramwell

All rights reserved.
No portion of this book may be reproduced, used or transmitted in any form, except brief quotations
in critical articles or reviews, without written permission of the publisher.

Free Run Creations, LLC
PO Box 12605, Raleigh, NC 27605
www.freeruncreations.com

Photography by **Joyce Bramwell**
Design and layout by **Chris Capellini**
Edited by **Kristie Bramwell**
Index by **Heidi Blough**

First printing, 2011

Printed by Global Interprint
Printed in China

ISBN 978-0-615-31456-3

*To my family, for your continued support and encouragement
throughout the writing of this book, and for the constant reaffirmation
that a good meal is one of life's most easily attained luxuries.*

- AND -

*To Steve & Shelly Friend and John Driscoll for your guidance
in the discovery of how great wine can be;
without your influences I might still be drinking plonk.*

ACKNOWLEDGMENTS

I am blessed to have many incredibly talented and artistically gifted people in my life who have helped to make VinoBurger something bigger and immeasurably better than I could have possibly imagined. Thanks to Jay Murrie, for contributing your invaluable experience, irreplaceable expertise and unique point of view. The book would not have been the same without your participation; to my Mom, Joyce Bramwell, for your tireless dedication in creating the best photographs imaginable; to Chris Capellini, *mon frère*, for the graphic design and layout of VinoBurger - it's not just the story, but how it's told, and VinoBurger is a better story because of your hard work; to Kristie Bramwell, my editor (who just happens to be my sister-in-law), who was willing to work in exchange for a lifetime supply of rosé… I just wish I knew how much you like rosé before I signed that deal; and to Todd Bramwell and Jeff Statile, for being a sounding board since day one.

Very special thanks to Todd & Kristie Bramwell, Amanda & Todd Kendrick and Ryan & Jenny Fulkerson for letting me destroy your kitchens on a regular basis while testing these recipes.

Thanks to the tasting panel for your participation and feedback: Todd, Kristie & Grace Bramwell, Steve & Shelly Friend, Amanda & Todd Kendrick, Mom & Dad, Ryan & Jenny Fulkerson, Erica Sanger, Matt & Cara Fulkerson, Jay & Megan Murrie, Nile Zacherle & Whitney Fisher Zacherle, Sheri Sauter Morano & Bill Morano, Jeff & Gina Statile, Chris & Tina Capellini, Nick Stroz, Mike Via, Ron & Marge Statile, Sean & Laurie Rubino, Chip & Jen Burmester, Seth Hoffman, Matt Fern, Lauren Deloatch, Rob Saliski, Bill & Mary Saliski, Dan & Allison Driver, Katie Hawthorn, Todd Hawthorn, Lori Ferguson, Dave & Chris Drap and Wendy Chapman.

Sincere thanks to the folks behind the wonderful wines that appear throughout VinoBurger: Blake Murdock at the Rare Wine Co; Nile Zacherle; Whitney Fisher Zacherle at Fisher Vineyards; Enzo Boglietti; Aldo Vacca at Produttori del Barbaresco; Fabio Chiarelotto at Montepeloso; Brian Bicknell and Dave Kenny at Mahi Wine; Matt Gant at First Drop Wines; Toni Soellner at Weingut Soellner; René Rostaing; Javier Izurieta at Pazo de Señorans; Alvaro Palacios; Doug Donovan and Claudia Sina at Vias Imports.

Additional thanks to Judy Jennings at Global Interprint, John Driscoll, Bill Bowman, Doug Diesing and the entire staff at Seaboard Wine, Kurt Saylor and everyone at The Wine Merchant, Susan Greene, Flowers Hoffler, Jennifer King, Andrea Fullbright, Brad Beavers, Cory Sloan, Toby Hooker, Jen Vieceli, Alex Gray, Rob & Rita Menzies, Adm. Leighton & Dottie Smith and Lonnie Jurenko.

FOREWORD

Crafting a burger can offer as much creative expression as turning grapes into wine. It can be as simple or complex as your palate prefers. I often enjoy a couple of burgers a week without fear of redundancy. As a winemaker and a passionate oenophile, I appreciate how a simple wine can deliver layers of flavor in the way that the purity of its grapes are revealed, and the same goes for a burger and its ingredients.

One often thinks the appropriate burger beverage is a beer, but when wine and burger meet something truly amazing can happen. Jeff Bramwell's book explores this concept with much precision and regional respect for both wine and food. He has brought the artisanal burger to a new level by pairing wines of classic regions with the flavor nuances of their native foods, each magnifying the satisfaction derived from the other. VinoBurger is as much about artisanal burgers as it is about wine, and it makes learning about both a delicious experience.

We often find ourselves cooking with friends and family while sharing a bottle or two of wine. I find it especially rewarding when the people around me get involved in what we are eating and drinking. VinoBurger offers a creative landscape to match these two crucial elements of a meal, while hopefully inspiring others to join in the experience.

VinoBurger will excite both your palate and your imagination, while offering a fresh new view at one of our favorite foods.

~ Nile Zacherle
Winemaker, Zacherle Wines

TABLE *of* CONTENTS

INTRODUCTION

With all the incredible, inspiring ingredients now readily available at most grocery stores, farmers' markets and gourmet food purveyors, why limit yourself to the standard burger combination of beef, lettuce, tomato, processed cheese and ketchup? Don't get me wrong, I'm not knocking the classic recipe. There's a reason it's an American institution. But our modern hamburger's origins can be traced back to Europe, so why not take it for an international spin and introduce some new flavors into your repertoire? And I see no reason not to combine America's favorite food with one of the world's favorite beverages. The result: VinoBurger! The recipes contained in this cookbook were created using ingredients authentic to each of the world's best winegrowing areas. You'll be able to find delicious wines from each of these regions at just about any good wine retailer in America.

The VinoBurger concept was born out of the simple joy I get from sharing a bottle of wine and some good food with friends and family. Creating recipes in the familiar form of a burger is a fun twist that makes the exploration of wine more enjoyable. It also makes the learning process a little less intimidating for those who are new to the subject. By opening several types of wine from a given region over the course of an evening, the whole experience becomes a sort of vinous travelogue. It also encourages even the most serious of wine aficionados to have fun while further exploring what each region has to offer.

VinoBurger is not intended to be an all-encompassing wine education, but I will give you a pretty detailed snapshot of the major grape varieties that grow in each region, the important sub-regions you're likely to encounter at your local wine merchant and an overall feel for a region. Of course I'll also provide suggestions of what wines to pair with your burgers.

VINOBURGER PRINCIPLES

All around the world, what grows together goes together, so pairing a wine to its local cuisine generally can't miss. In an effort to create the most enjoyable experience possible I followed a few guidelines I'd like to share:

AUTHENTICITY

Authenticity of flavor is the cornerstone of this cookbook. Each burger and side dish recipe was inspired by the culinary traditions of a specific winegrowing region. Sometimes I created the burger to emulate a specific dish closely associated with a particular place. More often, I created the recipe after compiling a list of ingredients commonly used in that region. In wine-speak, these recipes display *terroir*. On occasion, I take a little creative license and suggest an ingredient more widely available than, but very similar to, whatever is most authentic to a region. This is most prevalent with cheeses that are simply not readily available in the U.S. In most cases, I list the authentic ingredient as well as a common stand-in. However, when you do have the choice between the high-quality genuine article and an imitation, always choose the real thing. And fresh, local, in-season produce will always taste better than old veggies flown in from half a world away. I encourage you to eat globally, but source locally.

PREPARATION

Most of these are not your standard, middle-of-the-week burger recipes that are complete, start to finish, in half an hour. Nevertheless, I've simplified as much as possible some complex, time-consuming processes, such as sauce reductions. You'll find a brief overview of the time commitment for each recipe included in the Table Of Contents. As much as wine is intended to be appreciated leisurely rather than quickly gulped down, I suggest taking your time with the meal preparation. Have your dining companions help with the cooking, open a bottle to serve as a precursor to the meal, then open a different bottle to go with the burgers.

INGREDIENTS

Some traditional burger ingredients and toppings, like pickles, ketchup and barbecue sauce are not used because they generally don't pair well with most wines. I've also limited the use of certain ingredients to prevent too much repetition; a challenge, considering that virtually every culture embraces the fact that everything tastes better with bacon. For the sake of keeping things interesting, we'll delve deeper into a region's culinary traditions to create a more unique (but equally authentic) burger, sometimes foregoing the most obvious choice of ingredients. Additionally, it is rare to see a country or region that isn't influenced by its neighbors, so although you will see some similarities among a few burgers, each one has its own unique flavor spectrum.

Every good chef preaches using the best ingredients possible, and I hope that you'll prepare a Grand Cru version of these burgers using fresh herbs and spices, freshly-ground meat and in-season, local produce. Truth is, due to limitations of seasonal availability, budget and time constraints, you may need to take a shortcut from time to time. I can assure you the end product will still be great, but the Grand Cru version will easily be worth the extra effort.

WINE

I'm a firm believer that as long as you know what you like when you taste it, that's all that matters. Any extra-curricular reading you choose to do is a bonus, but not required for a casual appreciation of wine. See the Further Reading section for recommendations of some excellent wine-related books. But all that's required for the thorough enjoyment of VinoBurger is an open mind and a willingness to try wines and ingredients you may not be familiar with, or that you haven't necessarily loved in the past. Tastes constantly evolve, and you may love something now that you didn't care for a couple of years ago.

So, grab a glass of wine, flip through the recipes on the following pages, and decide which burger you want to make with your friends this weekend. Prost!

MEAT SELECTION AND PROCESSING

Everyone wants a juicy, flavorful burger. There's no way around it... juiciness comes from the fat content of the meat you're cooking. You simply can't make the perfect burger without at least a little bit of fat. Many meats – beef, pork, chicken, turkey, lamb and more – are frequently offered with a choice of fat content. When you have the option, buy the meat that has more fat, up to 20%. If you find a cookbook about delicious fat-free tofu burgers then you can make one of those tomorrow.

Processing the meat is an integral part of creating the tastiest burger imaginable. Whenever possible, take the additional three minutes to grind (or chop) the meat yourself. It will be fresher tasting and safer than pre-ground, as bacterial contamination is less of an issue when you're grinding your own meat. And because there is less concern about bacteria, you won't have to cook the burgers to as high an internal temperature as you should with pre-ground meat. Additionally, you can leave the burgers a little bit on the chunky side if you like, a huge plus when working with chicken and turkey since you won't need to add any (or at least not as many) breadcrumbs to create a manageable patty.

Below is a guide for finding and choosing the proper meat for your burger, along with directions for processing the meat, and substitution suggestions in case you can't find certain meats. If you grind your own beef, lamb, veal, pork or venison in a food processor you may find that a very small splash of olive oil helps bring everything together into an easier-to-form patty. On the flip side, when preparing chicken, turkey, duck or fish, you may need to use breadcrumbs to bind everything together.

BEEF

Beef is obviously easy to find at any grocery store or gourmet market, but you still have choices to make. Do you buy pre-ground, or do you have the time and equipment to grind it yourself? What cut do you use? If you can grind your own at home, try a combination of chuck roast, boneless short ribs, brisket or top sirloin. You can use dry-aged or grass-fed beef for an especially meaty taste, or try Wagyu beef for the most tender burger you can imagine. If you don't have a meat grinder, just cube the meat and pulse it in a food processor until sufficiently chopped, being careful not to over-process. If you must buy pre-ground meat, ground chuck with a fat content of 20% is easy to find, and makes a very good burger. Don't even think about buying frozen patties.

LAMB

When grinding your own, start with a lamb shoulder. Cut it into cubes and grind with a meat grinder or pulse in a food processor to the desired texture. Pre-ground lamb is becoming increasingly easy to find in better grocery stores and gourmet markets, but if you can't find it, beef is a good substitute.

VEAL

You will likely have less choice when selecting cuts for your own ground veal, so ask your butcher for the best cut available for grinding and grilling. Pre-ground veal is fairly easy to find, but you are less likely to have a choice of the fat content. If you can't find veal, try a mix of two parts beef and one part pork.

PORK

Grind your own pork using a shoulder cut, plus two to three ounces of pork fatback per pound of shoulder. If you're chopping the pork in a food processor, you'll want to process the fatback pretty thoroughly before adding in the cubed pork shoulder. Pre-ground pork is widely available, occasionally with several choices of fat content. Always use the higher fat content. Chicken is the most widely available and acceptable substitute on the rare occasion that you can't find pork.

CHICKEN & TURKEY

In both cases, dark meat is always the preferred choice over white meat, thanks to higher fat content and better flavor. My first choice, by far, is to work with boneless, skinless thigh meat when using chicken. You may not have any options besides breast meat when it comes to turkey. Cube the meat and pulse it in a food processor until it's just a little chunky, being very cautious not to over-process. Process your own and you may not even need to add any breadcrumbs, which is a plus. If you're using pre-ground chicken you can get away with adding fewer breadcrumbs to dark meat than you can with white meat. It's not the end of the world, but it changes the texture a little and the burger won't be as moist as when you don't use the breadcrumbs. Cooking in a cast iron pan set on a grill or on a stovetop is the recommended method. If the chicken or turkey patties hold together well enough then you can get away with grilling them.

DUCK

Duck breast is certainly not as easy to find as ground beef, but it's not as difficult as you may think. It's most frequently found in the freezer section of your local supermarket or at a gourmet grocery store. More often than not, I find it in packages of two breasts totaling twelve ounces. But beware, some are pre-marinated in flavors you won't want for these recipes. Duck presents a rare circumstance where it comes with more fat than is ideal. Buy enough duck so you can sacrifice some of the fat and still have enough meat for the recipe. For every two duck breasts I'm using, I like to remove and discard the fat layer from one breast, and leave the fat and skin on the other breast prior to chopping. To chop, thaw the duck completely, and cut into 1" cubes. Place the cubed duck meat in a food processor and pulse until it creates a lightly chunky texture. It's better to have it a little too chunky than to turn it into a paste. Work in batches if necessary. The coarser it is, the fewer breadcrumbs it'll take to hold together as a burger. There's really no ideal substitution that's any easier to find than duck, but in a pinch, pork will get the job done in most of these recipes.

VENISON

Like duck breast, you'll most likely find venison in the frozen foods section. If you can find it whole, cut it into cubes, and pulse in a food processor until it is fairly smooth, leaving some small chunks. Pre-ground is also pretty widely available if you know where to look for it. Substitute beef or lamb when you can't find venison.

TUNA & SALMON

First and foremost, always purchase your fish from a retailer you trust, both for freshness and for recommendations on what's best that day. Generally speaking, wild-caught is higher quality than farm-raised and fresh fish shouldn't smell fishy. When ordering your fish, have the skin removed to ensure you have enough flesh for your recipe.

For salmon, ask your fishmonger to remove the pin bones. When preparing the salmon, feel along the filet for any remaining pin bones, which are easily removed with a pair of needle-nose pliers.

To mince the fish, get a large chef's knife and cut the salmon fillet or tuna steak into 1" cubes and chop the fish until it is well minced. Work in batches if necessary to ensure an even texture. Alternately, a few pulses in a food processor will get the job done very quickly.

COOKING THE PERFECT BURGER

Quite simply, if you've ever cooked a burger before, then you can make every recipe in this book. The ingredients are different and the prep time is longer, but the recipes themselves are pretty easy, and the final product is absolutely worth the extra effort. Your biggest challenge will be to get the burgers on the grill at the right temperature, and then exercise restraint and let them cook without too much interference. Here are the rules for making the best burger possible:

1) Use the freshest meat possible. Whenever possible, purchase it the day you plan to use it and have your butcher grind it to order for you. Better yet, grind it yourself. In the case of burgers made with duck, tuna or salmon you'll have to process it yourself. See the previous section for more information on meat selection and processing.

2) Mix the burger ingredients as gently as possible or you'll run the risk of ending up with a dense, dry burger.

3) Form the patty with the same care you use when mixing the ingredients. Shape them according to the size of your burger bun, but remember they're going to shrink a bit during the cooking process. Once you've formed your burger patties, use your thumb to make an indentation in the middle of the burger. This will help prevent your burgers from shrinking into meatballs during the cooking process.

4) Whether you're cooking on a charcoal, gas or electric grill, or a stainless steel, cast iron or non-stick sauté pan, always let the cooking surface preheat to the proper cooking temperature before adding the burgers. If you're cooking over charcoal, get the fire started early enough so you can cook over proper, even heat. Brush your grill grates with a little vegetable oil, or add enough to a sauté pan to lightly coat the bottom. This will prevent the burgers from sticking to your cooking surface and it'll also help them brown perfectly. If your grill has uneven heat, set a cast iron skillet over the grates and preheat for at least fifteen minutes. Just before cooking, add a drizzle of vegetable oil to the skillet.

5) Once the burgers are on the cooking surface, just let them be. Don't even think about touching them for at least two minutes. If you're cooking in a pan, put the lid on, with a slight crack to let the steam out. If you're cooking on a grill, close it once the burgers are on the grates. After the first two minutes are up you can check the progress. Turn the burgers 45 degrees if you want those perfect grill marks, but leave them alone otherwise. When the first side has developed a good crust and the sides of the burger are starting to cook through, then you can flip 'em over. Don't even think about pushing down on them with your spatula…ever.

6) Use a meat thermometer to check the internal temperature of the burgers, and allow for about five degrees of carry-over cooking. If you're comfortable gauging the doneness by touch, a medium-rare to medium burger should have a decent bit of resistance, but certainly should not be firm. For a good approximation, make a lightly clenched fist; lightly push on the web of your hand between your thumb and index finger. Pull your burgers off the grill when they have that amount of resistance, and then...

7) Let your burgers rest five minutes before serving them. It's okay to put them on the bun and assemble the toppings during these five minutes, but don't cut or bite into them or you'll lose those juices.

The required internal cooking temperature varies depending on the type of meat you're preparing. Below is a guideline for internal temperatures according to the USDA. Once again, don't forget about carryover cooking!

INTERNAL TEMPERATURES

Tuna, Swordfish, Salmon..............................**145°**

Beef, Veal, Lamb, Pork, Venison....................**160°**

Chicken, Turkey, Duck..................................**165°**

THE PERFECT BURGER BUN

You've just mixed your ingredients together for the perfect burger, using the freshest ground meats, ripest produce, and the most fragrant herbs and spices available to you. You waited for the grill to get up to just the right temperature before gently placing the burgers on the grates. After cooking them to perfection, you let those burgers rest and turn your attention towards pouring the wine you selected to compliment the feast. So if you take this much care with the rest of the meal then why would you serve that perfect burger on just any old bun?

The burger bun plays a pivotal role in the creation of the perfect burger. Standard burger buns from the bread aisle are often too dense and dry. A crusty little French roll, ciabatta or bolillo roll might sound like a good choice, but the outside is usually too hard. You have to work to bite through it, causing the burger to slide around. And then when you do bite through, that crust dominates the softer texture of the burger and all those tasty toppings - creamy cheeses, crisp lettuce and crumbling bacon all suffer. Not to mention, the pressure that you exert on the burger while you're biting through the crust forces all those juices to squirt out, becoming a mess to eat. There's something to be said for a messy burger from time to time, but not when you're reaching for a wine glass.

As such, I'm very particular when I choose a bun for my burger. I'd love to have something authentic to the region of choice, but not if it gets in the way of the inherent deliciousness of the burger and the toppings. For me, the perfect bun is airy and pillow-soft to the touch. In addition to being a lot less dense, it's also a little smaller than the standard issue burger buns you find in the bread aisle, allowing you to form a slightly thicker, and therefore juicier, burger. The only time I reach for a wider bun is when I'm working with a burger that may not hold together quite as well as a beef burger, such as salmon and tuna, or when I know I'm piling on a lot of toppings, in which case I might go for a super-soft Kaiser roll. Spend a little extra time searching for the ideal, freshly baked bun and the entire burger will be better for it.

The treatment of the burger bun is up to your preferences; do you like the fluffy texture of a bun that was split just prior to serving? Or do you prefer them lightly toasted on the grill or under a broiler? How about browned in a small pool of butter on a hot skillet? All of these are good choices, so you won't see much instruction on what to do with the buns in the following recipes. Just make sure they're as fresh as the meat and produce you're buying.

DECODING WINE-SPEAK

While this book is not intended to provide a complete wine education, I strive to make the topic more enjoyable and easier to understand. For a comprehensive introduction to the process of tasting and assessing wine, look for Jancis Robinson's *How To Taste: A Guide to Enjoying Wine* or Andrea Immer Robinson's *Great Wine Made Simple*. Below is an explanation of a few key concepts, followed by a brief list of tasting terms that will help you to better communicate with your local wine merchant, sommelier and fellow wine drinkers.

BALANCE

The most important aspect of every wine is its flavor and how it's balanced by the wine's acidity, alcohol and, when applicable, tannin, sugar and barrel aging treatment. Even the most basic bottle of wine needs to have some semblance of balance, as a wine that has just one of these elements too far out of whack can be deemed undrinkable. Enthusiastic collectors stash away treasured bottles, seeking out that exact moment when all of those elements come into focus at the same time, revealing a whole that is greater than its parts.

Here is a summary of each of these components:

ACIDITY: In all wines, whether red, white or otherwise, an appropriate amount of acidity provides a freshness that keeps us coming back for another taste. Acidity also provides the backbone for a wine; too little of it and the wine can be described as "flat," "flabby" or "unfocused." Too much and the wine is referred to as "tart," "sharp" or "high-toned." A white wine that is supposed to show elevated levels of acidity, such as Sauvignon Blanc, may be described as "bright," "crisp," "racy" or even "nervy."

TANNIN: A type of acid, tannin is the mouth-drying, astringent quality of a red wine that provides structure for both present-day drinking and over the long haul. Tannin is extracted from the grape's skin, seeds and stems during maceration, the period during which these solids soak with the juice in the fermentation tank. When applicable, tannin can also be extracted from the barrel the wine ages in. Tannin is typically a non-factor with white wines because of their brief maceration times. A wine that is overly tannic may be described as "austere," with little fruit showing through to provide pleasurable drinking. Tannin softens over time and precipitates out of the wine in the form of sediment, so a wine that is austere in its youth may develop into something more enjoyable with age, but only if the fruit can outlive the tannin.

SUGAR: Unfermented sugar, or residual sugar, is covered in greater detail below. Simply put, sweetness throws a wine out of balance when it is readily apparent in a wine where it is not desired. Wines that are supposed to have residual sugar must also have proper accompanying acidity to balance the sweetness.

ALCOHOL: Alcohol is produced when yeast consumes sugar; the higher the sugar content in the grape when harvested, the higher the potential alcohol in the finished wine. While it is part of the reason we enjoy wine in the first place, alcohol is only welcome to the degree that the rest of the wine can contain it. Once it starts over-asserting itself, the wine becomes far less enjoyable and is described as being "hot."

BARREL AGING: The time a wine spends in barrel, if any, goes a long way to determining how it will taste once it goes into bottle. The type of wood, amount of toast on the barrel, number of times a particular barrel has been used and the time a wine spends in cask can have a broad range of effects on the finished wine. Flavors range from a subtle note of toasted bread to slightly more prominent vanilla and caramel notes, all the way to rich espresso and chocolate. Some winemakers choose to use a barrel to impart a subtle influence, meant only to enhance an already well-made wine. Others let it speak a little louder, while some go so far as to let the barrel dominate the wine's flavor profile.

SWEETNESS

The word "sweet" is the biggest troublemaker in the wine lexicon, as it carries several meanings. In its most literal meaning, a wine that is sweet contains a moderate amount of residual sugar (measured in grams per liter) that is left unfermented in the winemaking process. The majority of quality-made wine is dry or even bone-dry. Just a hint of residual sugar and a wine walks the line between dry and off-dry, making you question what to call it. White wines from Alsace can display this quality in a good way. Inexpensive, big production wines also have this tendency, in a not-so-pleasant way. Next are those wines that fall into the off-dry category. These wines have a perceptible – but not overwhelming – amount of residual sugar. German wines labeled "Kabinett" tend to provide a good example. As the sweetness of a wine increases, the integral balancing ingredient is acidity. A proper amount of acidity has the ability to prevent a sweet wine from teetering into "cloying" territory, where the sweetness gets to be heavy and clumsy on the palate, if not downright nauseating.

Now the gray area: a wine that is technically dry may display loads of ripeness, a quality that can lead even the most seasoned professionals to refer to that wine as being somewhat sweet. More accurately, these wines are intensely fruity – a term that tends to be a turn-off to many wine drinkers. Grapes that are allowed extended hang time on the vine become ever more ripe. This leads to big, robust fruit flavors, which come at the expense of those qualities that help to balance a wine's *perceived* sweetness - tannin and acid.

Barrel aging can also contribute to a wine's perceived sweetness. Before the wine is placed in the barrel, the interior of the barrel gets toasted over an open flame, creating varying levels of char. The vanilla, caramel, chocolate and coffee flavors that result from barrel aging imply sweetness without actually contributing any sugar content to the wine.

AGE-WORTHINESS

A wine's age-worthiness is tied to those individual components that are expected to mature together, creating a beverage more enjoyable in its later life than in its infancy. With enough experience, you'll notice that it is most frequently the tannin or acid - not the dollar amount - that determines a wine's ability to age gracefully.

A big distinction needs to be made when evaluating wines you intend to hold for more than a year or two: is this a wine that is expected to improve with age, or one that is expected to simply maintain its current quality over the course of a 3-, 5- or 10-year period? Either one is fine, depending on your preferences. But there are a lot of expensive wines out there that drink great when they're young and fall apart quickly thereafter because they lack the necessary qualities that provide balance over the long-term. Others are covered up with more oak than will ever be able to integrate into the wine before the fruit starts to fade. Acid, tannin, and in the case of dessert wines, sugar, are natural preservatives, so as you can imagine, if a wine lacks these qualities there is a rather finite shelf life.

NOTEWORTHY TASTING TERMS:

ANGULAR: Unbalanced. Usually used to refer to a wine in which either the tannin or the acidity is noticeably out of whack.

BODY: The heaviness or heft perceived on the palate that leads a wine to be called light-, medium- or full-bodied. In most quality table wines, the body is determined by the characteristics of the grape itself, rather than what might be done in the winemaking process. Light-bodied wines may be described as "delicate" or "subtle." Full-bodied wines can be referred to as "big," "structured" or "rich." An especially dense wine may be referred to as "extracted," "brooding" or "brawny."

BUTTERY: A wine that displays the distinct aroma of butter as a result of a process called malolactic fermentation, which converts malic acid (found in green apples) into lactic acid (found in dairy products). This is most common in full-bodied white wines such as Chardonnay, and tends to go hand in hand with barrel aging.

CLOSED OR DUMB: A wine that, for various reasons, offers up very little aroma or fruit flavor. Not uncommon for young, age-worthy wines.

COMPLEX: A wine that offers many layers of aromas and flavors.

CORKED: A wine that is flawed due to the presence of the chemical compound *2,4,6-trichloroanisole* (nearly always abbreviated "TCA"). A mildly affected wine's aromas may simply be muted, while more potent examples give off aromas of wet cardboard, wet dog, moldy newspaper or cork itself. There is no harm in consuming a corked wine, but there is also little joy. Approximately 8% of all cork-sealed wines are affected, from one degree to another, by TCA. Screw caps aren't looking so bad, are they?

EARTHY: Soil-like aromas that may be accompanied by notes of wet or dry leaves or mushrooms.

FAT: Ripe and rich, but balanced.

FLABBY: Lacking acidity. Unfocused.

FLAWED: A wine that has a technical defect, beyond what could be chalked up to a person's preferences. A wine that is "corked" is the most frequent flaw (see above). Other common flaws include volatile acidity (vinegary smell and taste), *brettanomyces* contamination (wet dog and sweaty aromas), sulphur (rotten egg or burnt match aroma), and secondary fermentation (effervescence in a wine that shouldn't be fizzy; unappealing yeasty flavor).

GREEN OR HERBACEOUS: A vegetal, under-ripe aroma. Generally not a complimentary term.

HOLLOW: A wine that is thin or watery.

LENGTH: The duration in which you can taste the wine's flavors after you have swallowed.

MINERALITY: An elusive tasting descriptor, minerality is often likened to crushed rocks or wet stones, not far off from being chalky. It's easiest to find minerality in high-acid, unoaked wines from cool-climate regions. Try a good Chablis or Sancerre for top examples.

OAKY/WOODY: An overt oak/wood influence. As with almost every aspect of wine, proper wood influence is a matter of taste.

POLISHED: A wine with soft tannins and mild acidity. No rough edges. Easy drinking.

PRIMARY: A simple, un-evolved wine that shows very little complexity. An acceptable quality found in inexpensive wines or in age-worthy wines when they are very young. A negative quality when speaking of a mature wine that was expected to evolve into something special.

ROASTED: Over-ripe, raisiny notes. Sometimes referred to as "cooked" or "stewed" as a result of grapes that were allowed to hang too long on the vine. A wine that has roasted qualities usually has high alcohol and low acidity.

ROUND: Well balanced, with relatively soft tannins and acid.

SILKY OR SUPPLE: A lush texture, with soft tannins and acid. Similar to "round" or "polished."

TERROIR: All the natural elements, such as soil composition, topography and climate of the region the grapes are grown in, that impact the wine's characteristics. Theoretically, every patch of dirt that yields grapes (or any other produce, for that matter) is capable of expressing its highly specific place of origin. If a winemaker takes a minimalist approach, a number of vintages of the same wine should show a common thread running throughout; a blueprint that is evident from one year to the next, complimented by the unique qualities imparted by the climatic differences in any given year.

TIRED: A wine that is past its prime. The fruit – along with everything else – has faded, offering little flavor.

VARIETALLY CORRECT: A wine that displays the characteristics expected of the grape it is made from. For example, a Pinot Noir that is too big and shows an overwhelming amount of dark fruits rather than cherry or raspberry would be described as lacking varietal correctness. Whether this is a detractor or not is completely subjective.

FRANCE

French wine can be maddeningly confusing to the burgeoning oenophile, thanks to its seemingly limitless number of appellations, vast list of grape varieties and, most daunting, the unfathomable wine labels. However, France is indisputably responsible for a staggering number of the world's greatest wines, making it a highly worthwhile subject of exploration, no matter how faint of heart one may be.

French wines are almost always labeled according to their place of origin rather than their grape content (Alsace being the most notable exception). The Appellation d'Origine Contrôlée, or AOC, is a place-name used in France for wine and other agricultural items, intended to guarantee that a region's products comply with government-enforced regulations. This system ensures that a wine bearing an AOC place-name will be made only from specific grapes grown in that region. However, it does little to guarantee the quality of the product.

The AOC listed on a label will zero in on the smallest, most specific place in which all the grapes are grown. Sometimes that may encompass an entire region, such as Burgundy, while other times it may narrow the area down to a single village (Vosne-Romanée) or even a single vineyard (La Tâche) which may be listed in addition to, or in place of, a village name. Depending on the region, the best vineyards may be accompanied by the term Grand Cru or Premier Cru (abbreviated 1er Cru). These are AOC-enforced designations, so, in theory, they should offer some of the best quality within a particular region. However, not every region in France has this classification system.

While browsing the shelves of your favorite wine shop, you'll likely encounter bottles that bear the term Indication Géographique Protégée (or IGP), which, as of 2009, has replaced the Vin de Pays classification. This designation, which excludes a wine from carrying an AOC name, allows a winemaker to include whatever grape varieties he or she chooses and allows those wines to be varietally-labeled. These wines usually offer lesser quality, but sometimes better value, than AOC wines from the same general area.

Of course, you can't learn French wine in a weekend, so the trick is to take it in small pieces. In the pages that follow, I cover the eight major regions you will encounter most frequently in wine stores and on restaurant wine lists. Learn those, and you'll be on your way to understanding French wine.

CHAMPAGNE

There's a lot of irony when it comes to Champagne. This magical beverage is held in such high esteem that most people reserve it for celebrations, yet its signature sparkle was considered a flaw when the wine was first created. No other drink carries such a strong sentiment of *joie de vivre*, yet its very birthplace has been repeatedly ravaged during periods of military conflict, particularly during World Wars I and II. Perhaps most ironic, there may not be a more food-friendly beverage on the planet, yet this joyous drink is often relegated to the role of aperitif, if not ignored completely.

Champagne's appeal is nearly universal. The mere pop of the cork induces a Pavlovian response that primes our taste buds for the first sip. The wine's brightly acidic tingle serves as the perfect tease for a bite of food. It pairs with just about everything, and the simplest of meals are all the more enjoyable when accompanied by a bottle of bubbly.

Champagne is the most imitated wine in the world. So what sets it apart from any other sparkling wine? Terroir has everything do with it. Champagne is a large region of northern France, roughly 100 miles northeast of Paris. Its cool climate and chalk-rich soils make this area prime territory for the creation of stellar sparkling wine. While the name has been co-opted and fraudulently used to sell bubbly by wineries from Barcelona to California, Champagne is a real place, a protected appellation, and its authentic wines have a character and quality rarely achieved elsewhere.

Real Champagne starts its life as a blend of still white wines, made from Chardonnay grapes and the gentle pressing of two black grapes, Pinot Noir and Pinot Meunier, which release only the clear juice held within. Most rosé Champagne gets its color from a splash of still red wine. These non-sparkling wines are exceedingly tart, the vinous equivalent of nails on a chalkboard. But this austerity allows the wine to retain finesse and elegance following its transformation into the product that we all know and love. Wines made elsewhere using the Méthode Champenoise can offer fantastic results, but they're just not the same as the best that come from this community of French farmers.

CHAMPAGNE

The reputation of Champagne was built on the success of the large producers, or "houses" as they're called here, but they have always been dependent upon the local growers who farm roughly 75,000 acres of vines spread across five sub-regions. Within these regions, it is the best villages – not the vineyards – that may be awarded Grand Cru or Premier Cru status.

In Montagne de Reims, the hillsides closest to the cathedral city of Reims are most closely associated with Pinot Noir, and the finest Blanc de Noirs (white wine made from black grapes) more often than not hail from this region. Just to the south, the Côte des Blancs is Champagne's epicenter for Chardonnay. The archetypes emanate from here; the truly amazing, racy, chalk-laden Blanc de Blancs that, one could argue, may be the world's greatest Chardonnay-based wines. To the east of the Côte de Blancs, the Vallée de la Marne may be a less-revered fruit source, but memorable wines come from top sites like Clos des Goisses. Pinot Meunier, a workhorse grape throughout much of Champagne, plays a major role here. Located in the southernmost part of Champagne's growing area, the Côtes de Sézanne and the Aube may not be loaded with Grand Crus, but they are home to many brand-name Champagne makers and ambitious small farmers who are bottling their own more affordable, character-filled wines.

The cost of producing wine in the Méthode Traditionelle is considerable, so even basic, non-vintage brut is likely to part you with about $40. A step up in quality has you looking at vintage-dated bottlings, Blanc de Blancs, Blanc de Noirs and some fine rosés. As with the best wine in any region, prestige cuvée Champagne can be a real bank-breaker. But there's no denying the excitement of popping the cork on a bottle of genuine article Champagne, so don't fear spending a few bucks to get a truly singular wine that's capable of turning any normal day into a special event. After all, without the occasional indulgence in a bottle of top-flight bubbly, the world would seem a cold, inhospitable place.

MAJOR WHITE GRAPES:

Chardonnay

MAJOR RED GRAPES:

Pinot Noir

Pinot Meunier

NOTEWORTHY VILLAGES:

Ambonnay

Avize

Ay

Bouzy

Verzenay

Verzy

Chouilly

Cramant

Le Mesnil-sur-Oger

Oger

Dizy

Epernay

Reims

CHAMPAGNE

We begin the VinoBurger experience with a bit of an outlier; despite Champagne's unquestioned standing as one of the world's important wine regions, it is somewhat lacking a signature cuisine. This section's inspiration comes from three major styles of Champagne - blanc de blancs, blanc de noirs, and rosé. So instead of a single recipe, I've created three different 'sliders' based on foods that pair famously well with each style. But rest assured, they are all flexible enough to pair with the full range of Champagne in any style, from basic brut non-vintage to rare prestige cuvées.

Though any one of these recipes is perfectly suitable for four regular-sized burgers, I suggest serving all three slider-sized mini burgers at your next dinner party.

RECOMMENDED COOKING METHOD: *Large cast iron skillet*
EACH RECIPE YIELDS: *4 normal sized burgers or 8 - 12 mini burgers*

BLANC DE BLANCS BURGER INGREDIENTS:

1 ½ lbs ground turkey, preferably dark meat
¼ cup finely chopped fennel
1 tbsp finely chopped tarragon
1 tsp salt
½ tsp ground black pepper
Breadcrumbs as needed

ASSEMBLE WITH:

Silver dollar rolls, split
Swiss cheese slices
1 fennel bulb, thinly sliced
Mayonnaise

BLANC DE NOIRS BURGER INGREDIENTS:

1 ¼ lbs ground veal
¼ cup finely diced celery
¼ cup crumbled feta cheese
1 tsp salt
½ tsp ground black pepper

SAUTÉED MUSHROOMS AND PROSCIUTTO:

1 tbsp olive oil
4 oz lightly chopped mushrooms
4 slices prosciutto, roughly chopped

ASSEMBLE WITH:

Silver dollar rolls, split
Sautéed mushrooms and prosciutto
Alfalfa sprouts
Feta cheese crumbles
Sour cream

ROSÉ BURGER INGREDIENTS:

1 ¼ lbs finely chopped duck breast (five duck breasts, fat and skin removed from three)

2 tbsp Dijon mustard

1 tsp salt

½ tsp ground black pepper

Breadcrumbs as needed

DIJON VINAIGRETTE:

2 tbsp bacon drippings

1 large shallot, thinly sliced

½ cup white wine

2 tbsp Dijon mustard

2 tbsp white wine vinegar

ASSEMBLE WITH:

Silver dollar rolls, split

8 slices bacon

Chaource, Camembert or Brie cheese

Dijon vinaigrette

SIDE DISH CHEESE PLATE:

Cheese plate: Blue cheese, Brie, aged goat cheese

Selection of crackers

Marcona almonds

POPCORN WITH TRUFFLE OIL:

½ cup popcorn kernels

3 tbsp vegetable oil, for popping

2 tsp truffle oil

Salt to taste

CHAMPAGNE

TO PREPARE

1. **Combine** *Blanc de Blanc* **burger ingredients** - Gently mix turkey, fennel, tarragon, salt and pepper in a mixing bowl. Add breadcrumbs as needed until turkey no longer sticks to your hand. Form into patties according to the size of the burger buns. Refrigerate until you are ready to cook.

2. **Combine** *Blanc de Noir* **burger ingredients** - Gently mix veal, celery, feta, salt and pepper in a mixing bowl. Form into patties according to the size of the burger buns. Refrigerate until you are ready to cook.

3. **Combine** *Rosé* **burger ingredients** - Remove and discard fat and skin from three of the five duck breasts. Cut the duck into 1-inch cubes, and pulse in a food processor until no large chunks remain, but not to a paste. Gently mix duck, Dijon mustard, salt and pepper in a mixing bowl. Add breadcrumbs as needed until the duck no longer sticks to your hand. Form into patties according to the size of the burger buns. Refrigerate until you are ready to cook.

4. **Gather buns and toppings, set aside. Make sure they are separated out accordingly for each burger so you're ready to top the burgers quickly once you take them off the grill.**

COOK & SERVE

1. **Sauté mushrooms and prosciutto** - Set a sauté pan over medium-high heat with 1 tablespoon of olive oil. Add mushrooms and cook until they begin to caramelize lightly. Add the prosciutto and cook an additional 2 minutes. Set aside.

2. **Cook bacon for *Rosé* burgers** - Cook 8 slices of bacon in a large sauté pan. Reserve 2 tablespoons of the bacon drippings for step 3.

3. **Make Dijon vinaigrette** - Sauté the shallots in the bacon drippings and cook over medium heat until they just barely start to caramelize. Add the white wine, Dijon mustard and white wine vinegar. Stir and reduce heat to medium-low. Simmer until the mixture has reduced down to the consistency of the mustard. Set aside.

4. **Assemble the side dishes** - Heat 3 tablespoons of vegetable oil in a large heavy-bottomed pot or stockpot over medium-high heat. Add the popcorn kernels and cover with a lid. With the lid still on, and using potholders, shake the pan every 15-20 seconds until popping stops. Transfer to a large bowl and toss with truffle oil and salt.

Serve the cheese plate along with a selection of crackers and a bowl of Marcona almonds or other nuts.

5. **Preheat a large cast iron pan or skillet on a 375° grill or on a stovetop burner set to medium-high heat. Drizzle the pan with vegetable oil just before adding burgers.**

6. **If serving as separate courses, cook the Blanc de Blancs burgers first, followed by the Blanc de Noirs burgers and finally the Rosé burgers. Cook burgers 2 to 3 minutes per side, or until cooked to preferred doneness.**

Add Swiss cheese to the *Blanc de Blancs* burger during final minute of cooking.

If you're serving all burgers at the same time, start cooking the Rosé burgers first, as they may take a minute longer than the others.

7. **Top burgers and serve on separate platters, along with a bottle each of the appropriate Champagne.**

Blanc de Blancs

Blanc de
Noirs

CHAMPAGNE

	Style:	*Grape(s):*
Sparkling:	Brut non-vintage	Chardonnay, Pinot Noir, Pinot Meunier
	Blanc de Blancs	Chardonnay
	Blanc de Noirs	Pinot Noir, Pinot Meunier
	Rosé	Pinot Noir, Pinot Meunier, Chardonnay

Vintage-dated Champagne may be made in any of the above styles and is typically produced only in exceptional years.

"Cuvée de prestige" is the top offering from a given Champagne house and may be made in any of the above styles.

Other great sparkling wines from around the world:

Crémant from France

Cava from Spain

Sparklers from Franciacorta in Lombardy, Italy

The best sparklers from California and Oregon

Sekt from Germany and Austria

Prosecco from the Veneto, Italy

Demi-sec Champagne

ALSACE

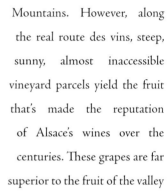

Alsace is a region of northeastern France, east of Lorraine and immediately west of the Rhine, bordering Germany and Switzerland. For centuries, military conflict caused control of the region to flip-flop between France and Germany, most recently back to France in late 1944. The result is a blurring of the lines in Alsace's culture, combining German and French influences, evident in its food and wine.

Viticultural Alsace is a thin, straight strip running 100 kilometers from Strasbourg in the north to Mulhouse in the south. The low, green Vosges Mountains to the west block much inclement weather and keep Alsace the driest wine-growing region of France. Fewer vine pests and fungal problems arise in comparison to the rest of the country, allowing Alsace's grape growers a greater ability to farm their vineyards organically. The region is home to many of the most vocal and universally admired members of the biodynamic farming movement.

It is surprising how much acreage is planted along the highway, between outcroppings of suburban Colmar and next to vegetable gardens far from the Vosges Mountains. However, along the real route des vins, steep, sunny, almost inaccessible vineyard parcels yield the fruit that's made the reputation of Alsace's wines over the centuries. These grapes are far superior to the fruit of the valley floor. Since Roman times, *vignerons* – or winemakers – of Alsace have known this, but recent global demand for Alsatian wines, facilitated by embarrassingly high permissible yields-per-acre, sent growers scurrying down from the hills and onto the plain. On a positive note, winemakers who stuck to their principles were able to expand holdings in the hills as these hard-to-farm sites were left fallow, including Alsace's best Grand Cru vineyards. Admittedly, the Grand Cru classification, which is currently awarded to 51 vineyards, was thrown together somewhat haphazardly starting in the early 1980s, and updated a decade later. Riesling, Muscat, Pinot Gris and Gewürztraminer are the only grapes that can be used in Grand Cru wines (the exception: Sylvaner is allowed in one Grand Cru, Zotzenberg). In a region known for unblended, varietally-labeled wines, blends are strangely permitted in a select few Grand Crus.

Riesling is undoubtedly king in Alsace, where it achieves ethereal highs. Dry, minerally, and packed with floral aromatics, the best wines of Alsace have attracted a following as frantically devoted as those of Bordeaux and Burgundy, albeit in far smaller numbers. It is the quintessential "wine-nerd" wine: high in acid, hardly ever oaked, heady in aromatic quality, highly expressive of its terroir, and an excellent companion to a diverse range of foods. As a result, it is a favorite among sommeliers.

Of course, Alsace is no one-trick pony. Gewürztraminer surely isn't lacking in personality, with a unique nose of spice, lychee nuts and rose petals, all wrapped around a slightly oily texture that makes it a popular pairing for Asian cuisine. Pinot Gris and Muscat round out the nobility of Alsatian varieties, while Pinot Blanc and Sylvaner follow close behind. The Klevner grape makes an appearance in sparkling Crémant d'Alsace, which is among the country's highest quality, wallet-friendly alternatives to Champagne. Pinot Noir, when it can be found, tends to be at its lightest when grown in Alsace, bordering on rosé territory. All these wines make for ideal pairings with the region's hearty cuisine.

MAJOR WHITE GRAPES:

Riesling

Gewürztraminer

Pinot Blanc

Pinot Gris

Sylvaner

MAJOR RED GRAPES:

Pinot Noir

NOTEWORTHY GRAND CRU VINEYARDS:

Rangen

Schlossberg

Furstentum

Goldert

Brand

Hengst

Rosacker

ALSACE

The Alsace Burger combines several of those ever-so-satisfying staples from the region's hearty cuisine. Choucroute, or sauerkraut, was enthusiastically adopted from neighboring Germany and incorporated into the Alsatian culinary repertoire. Pork is popular in all forms, so it's mixed with green apple here to form the burger, then gets topped with a couple of slices of smoky bacon for good measure. Gently melted Muenster cheese and a dab of mayonnaise finish it off, along with a helping of roasted potato wedges dusted with ground caraway seed.

RECOMMENDED COOKING METHOD: *Grill*   YIELDS: *4 servings*

BURGER INGREDIENTS:

1 ¼ lbs ground pork

½ cup finely chopped green apple

2 tsp ground fennel seed

1 tsp ground caraway seed

2 tsp lightly chopped sage

1 tsp salt

½ tsp ground black pepper

ASSEMBLE WITH:

4 burger buns, split

Muenster cheese slices

Sauerkraut

4 – 8 slices bacon

Mayonnaise

SIDE DISH CARAWAY ROASTED POTATO WEDGES:

1 ½ lbs russet potatoes

3 tbsp olive oil

2 tsp ground caraway seed

1 tsp salt

TO PREPARE

1. **Prep potatoes** - Rinse potatoes, and cut into wedges no thicker than a ½-inch. Place on a baking sheet and toss with olive oil, ground caraway seed and salt.

2. **Combine burger ingredients** - Gently mix pork, green apple, fennel seed, caraway seed, sage, salt and pepper in a large mixing bowl. Form burgers and set aside.

3. **Gather buns and toppings, set aside.**

COOK & SERVE

1. **Roast potatoes** - Heat oven to 350˚. Roast potatoes 40 minutes, flipping mid-way through cooking. Remove when potatoes are cooked through and evenly browned.

2. **Cook bacon** - Cook 1 to 2 slices per burger in large sauté pan.
Sauté sauerkraut in bacon drippings until warmed through (optional).

3. **Heat grill to 400˚.**

4. **Grill burgers 3 to 4 minutes per side, or until cooked to preferred doneness. Add Muenster during final 30 seconds of cooking.** .

5. **Serve, topping burgers with bacon, sauerkraut and mayonnaise.**

ALSACE

Alsatian wines are among the few in France that list the grape variety on the label. Below are the wines you are most likely to encounter at your local wine shop.

Sparkling: Crémant d'Alsace, most frequently made with Pinot Blanc, Pinot Gris, Pinot Noir and Riesling

White: Riesling

Pinot Blanc

Gewürztraminer

Pinot Gris

Sylvaner

Auxerrois Blanc

Muscat

Chasselas

White blends, called Edelzwicker

Red: Pinot Noir

ALTERNATE PAIRINGS

Most wines from Oregon, particularly whites

Australian Riesling

Whites and lighter-bodied reds from northern Italy

APPROPRIATE DESSERT WINE

Sélection de Grains Nobles, made from Gewürztraminer, Pinot Gris, Riesling or Muscat grapes affected by *Botrytis cinerea.*

LOIRE

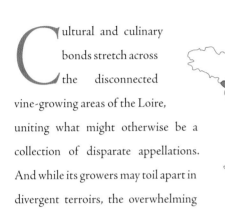

Cultural and culinary bonds stretch across the disconnected vine-growing areas of the Loire, uniting what might otherwise be a collection of disparate appellations. And while its growers may toil apart in divergent terroirs, the overwhelming *douceur*, the sweetness of life, along France's greatest river unites its *vignerons*. They live in the garden of France, and their life's work adds to the cumulative richness of this land. As the wide, slow Loire flows past innumerable Renaissance châteaux, ancient monasteries, pretty churches and historic towns with roots in the wine trade, the details may change, but the good life prevails.

In the recent past, the wines of the Loire's famous wine-growing regions were present in the U.S. mostly in the form of bottles from large-scale *négociants*, or brokers. They merely hinted at the character of the regions whose recognizable names pushed sales. In most instances, these bulk wines sold short the quality possible from places like Vouvray, Chinon, and Sancerre. Wines from lesser-known AOCs along the Loire simply did not exist in American stores at that time.

By the 1980s a small group of American wine importers were working hard to bring a better representation of these bottles stateside. Today, a good specialty wine shop can fill its shelves with a vast selection of wines from the Loire; bottlings from a diverse collection of farmers making white, rosé, red and sparkling wines in every conceivable style. Across its 50-plus appellations and 200,000 acres of vines, the Loire now offers perhaps the finest Chenin Blanc, Cabernet Franc and Sauvignon Blanc in the world. It's a place on the leading edge of winemaking in France, whose growers paradoxically have reached the forefront by taking a step back from "modern" equipment, instead opting for low-tech, honest farming to achieve the best possible product. These practices are very much a part of the region's storied past, an era when the Loire was a supplier of great wine to the restaurants of Paris and beyond.

On the edge of the Atlantic, surrounding the city of Nantes, vineyards are used primarily for the production of Muscadet, a dry white made of the Melon de Bourgogne grape. The best examples are bottled directly off the lees, or spent yeast cells that settle to the bottom of tanks after alcoholic fermentation. The *sur lie* bottling process creates texture and depth in wines that otherwise can be a touch neutral in character. Across France, Muscadet is the traditional accompaniment to mussels or oysters.

Anjou-Saumur makes wines of every color and almost every style, but, more than anything else, it is a region of great Chenin Blanc. The singular, amazing dry whites of Savennières have made this ancient royal province an exceptional source for Chenin Blanc, rivaled only by neighboring Touraine. Very good reds are made here too, most notably in Saumur and Saumur-Champigny.

In the Touraine, earthy, herbal Cabernet Franc from the Chinon and Bourgueil appellations offer great appeal to those whose palates veer away from the mainstream. Along the eastern boundary of Tours, the climate cools and Chenin Blanc dominates in Vouvray. The grape may be grown around the world, but the aromas of quince, honey and flowers that are found in many great Vouvrays, whether dry or sweet, create the archetype for Chenin. Across the river, Chenins from Montlouis show the capacity to eclipse the wines of their famous neighbor, should Vouvray falter.

In the easternmost extreme of the Loire Valley, Sancerre and Pouilly-Fumé yield Sauvignon Blanc of, arguably, the world's absolute highest quality. Sancerre has a particularly large amount of limestone and marl in its soils; great geology for crafting mineral-driven white wines. For the quality and bargain conscious, the "satellite" appellations Quincy and Menetou-Salon offer very enjoyable Sauvignon at a fraction of the price.

Wines of the Loire are particularly well-suited to warm weather and lighter cuisine, and one could do a lot worse than to have a variety of these refreshing selections on hand for when the mood strikes. Fortunately, these wines offer great bang for the buck, so it won't break the bank to stock the wine rack.

MAJOR WHITE GRAPES:

Sauvignon Blanc

Chenin Blanc

Melon de Bourgogne

MAJOR RED GRAPES:

Cabernet Franc

Gamay

NOTEWORTHY SUB-REGIONS:

Sancerre

Pouilly-Fumé

Vouvray

Muscadet

Savennières

Chinon

Bourgueil

Saumur

Anjou

The Loire Valley may be the "Garden of France," but that doesn't mean you're going to be stuck with some dry, flavorless veggie burger. Pork is popular here, so it's the starting point for this burger. The Loire is also the birthplace of beurre blanc, one of the world's great sauces, which I whip with goat cheese. Meaty chanterelle mushrooms sautéed with a handful of leeks give great depth of flavor, allowing the burger to pair with the valley's diverse whites, rosés and reds.

RECOMMENDED COOKING METHOD: *Grill*   YIELDS: *4 servings*

BURGER INGREDIENTS:

1 ½ lbs ground pork

¼ cup grated carrot

1 tsp salt

½ tsp ground black pepper

BEURRE BLANC WHIPPED GOAT CHEESE:

1 cup dry white wine

2 tbsp minced shallot

2 tbsp chilled butter

4 oz fresh goat cheese at room temperature

SAUTÉED LEEKS & CHANTERELLE MUSHROOMS:

3 oz fresh chanterelle mushrooms or ¾ oz dried

½ cup sliced leeks, white part only

2 tbsp butter

ASSEMBLE WITH:

4 burger buns, split

Sautéed leeks & chanterelle mushrooms

Beurre blanc whipped goat cheese

SIDE DISH MÂCHE SALAD:

4 cups mâche lettuce

1 Anjou pear, cored and sliced

4 slices bacon, thinly sliced

¼ cup sliced shallot

¼ cup dried cherries

3 tbsp red wine vinegar

Salt and pepper to taste

TO PREPARE

1. **If dried, rehydrate chanterelles** in a bowl of warm water for 30 minutes. Drain and set aside.

2. **Combine burger ingredients** - Gently mix pork, carrot, salt and pepper in a large mixing bowl. Form burgers and set aside.

3. **Gather buns and toppings, set aside.**

COOK & SERVE

1. **Make beurre blanc whipped goat cheese** - To make the beurre blanc, combine white wine and shallots in a sauté pan over medium heat. Cook until wine has reduced to about 1 tablespoon. Turn burner down to lowest setting and remove pan from heat. Add in butter a little bit at a time, and stir until butter is melted. You can put the pan back on the heat very briefly, warming the pan just enough to aid the gentle melting of the butter. As soon as butter has melted, combine beurre blanc with goat cheese in a small bowl. Set aside.

2. **Sauté chanterelles and leeks** - Place a large sauté pan on medium-high heat. Add butter and chanterelle mushrooms. Stir occasionally until chanterelles are lightly browned. Add sliced leeks, cooking until they are just barely soft. Remove from heat and set aside.

3. **Assemble salad** - Cook sliced bacon in a medium sauté pan. Once fat has rendered out and bacon begins to crisp up, add shallot and dried cherries and sauté until cherries begin to plump up. Add red wine vinegar and cook an additional 30 seconds. Remove from heat.

Place 1 cup of mâche lettuce on each plate, topped with sliced pear. While burgers are resting, top with bacon-shallot-cherry dressing and season with salt and pepper.

4. **Heat grill to 400°.**

5. **Grill burgers 3 to 4 minutes per side, or until cooked to preferred doneness.**

6. **Serve, topping burgers with sautéed leeks and chanterelles and beurre blanc goat cheese.**

LOIRE

TRADITIONAL PAIRINGS

	Noteworthy AOCs:	Grape(s):
Sparkling:	Vouvray and Saumur Mousseux	Chenin Blanc
	Crémant de Loire	Various
White:	Sancerre, Pouilly-Fumé, Quincy	Sauvignon Blanc
	Vouvray, Savennières, Saumur	Chenin Blanc
	Muscadet	Melon de Bourgogne
	Anjou	Chenin Blanc, Sauvignon Blanc, Chardonnay
	Touraine	Sauvignon Blanc, Chenin Blanc
Rosé:	Anjou	Cabernet Franc
	Touraine	Gamay, Cabernet Franc, Pinot Noir
Red:	Bourgueil, Chinon and Anjou	Cabernet Franc
	Sancerre	Pinot Noir
	Touraine	Gamay, Cabernet Franc, Pinot Noir

ALTERNATE PAIRINGS

Picpoul de Pinet from the Languedoc region of France

White wines from Slovenia

White wines from Bordeaux, France

APPROPRIATE DESSERT WINE

Vouvray moelleux or Quarts-de-Chaume, made from Chenin Blanc

BORDEAUX

Bordeaux is big, both literally and figuratively. It is the world's largest fine wine producing region, with over 300,000 acres of vines planted around the Gironde, Dordogne and Garonne rivers. Ten thousand producers bottle over sixty million cases of wine annually.

Quality is all over the map, but the top two-dozen or so estates are unquestionably among the finest in the world. These châteaux produce the blue-chip wines that garner more attention than any others, from critics, collectors and auction houses alike. They craft the archetype that has inspired similarly-styled wines around the world.

Ninety percent of the wine made in Bordeaux is red; almost invariably a blend of predominantly Cabernet Sauvignon and/or Merlot. Cabernet Franc occasionally asserts itself as a significant player, while Petite Verdot and Malbec show up in small percentages, principally for the intense color they contribute. Semillon, Sauvignon Blanc and Muscadelle are the white grapes of choice, two-thirds of which are made into dry wine, with the balance made into dessert wine.

Grape varieties are planted to match the soil of the gently rolling landscape. The "Left Bank," or western bank, of the Gironde River is composed of a high proportion of gravel, which provides ideal drainage for Cabernet Sauvignon vines. This northwesterly portion of Bordeaux forms the Médoc growing area, with the finest châteaux located in the AOCs of Pauillac, Margaux, Saint-Estèphe and Saint-Julien. Further south, in Pessac-Léognan and the larger Graves area, the gravel content is even higher, lending stony minerality to a fairly even split of Cabernet Sauvignon and Merlot. Bordeaux's dry white wine production reaches its pinnacle here; Semillon takes the lead in Graves while Sauvignon Blanc plays a larger role in Pessac-Léognan. Some of the world's finest dessert wines are made in Sauternes and neighboring Barsac, both sub-appellations of Graves.

Along the Dordogne River, south of the vast Côtes de Blaye, Côtes du Bourg and Bordeaux Supérieur lay the outstanding appellations of Saint-Emilion and Pomerol. The clay-dominated soil of the "Right Bank" makes this Merlot territory. Both at home and

BORDEAUX

abroad, this oft-maligned grape is made into unmemorable wine. But in the right hands it can achieve wondrous success, and nowhere but in Bordeaux is this so readily evident. The best come from small producers in Saint-Emilion and tiny Pomerol, but solid examples are found in the less pedigreed "satellite appellations" of Côtes de Castillon, Lalande-de-Pomerol and Fronsac.

Bordeaux has enjoyed greater global success with its wines than most other regions around the world. This is due in part to the long-standing support of the British. Eleanor of Aquitaine and Henry II of England were married in the twelfth century, paving the way for Bordeaux wines to be imported into England. Since then, minus wartime interruptions, the British have been enthusiastic consumers of Bordeaux's clarets. These wines received even greater attention in 1855 during the Exposition Universelle, held in Paris, for which Napoleon requested a classification of the region's wines be drawn up. Bordeaux's négociants ranked the top sixty-one châteaux producing dry red wine, and separated them into five tiers, called *crus* (growths), according to prestige and selling price. The classification, which remains largely unchanged today, focused on the châteaux of the Médoc, plus Haut-Brion in Graves. At the same time, those négociants created a separate classification for the sweet whites of Sauternes and Barsac. Since then, the powers-that-be in Saint-Emilion and Graves have created their own classifications, while Pomerol has not.

So, how does it taste? At its finest, Bordeaux is the unquestioned prototype of both Cabernet Sauvignon and Merlot world-wide, delivering power and complexity in spades. A new style of Bordeaux has emerged over the past thirty years, as greater control and refinement in the cellar has allowed for the better taming of tannin and the accentuation of fruit. Regardless, dark cassis fruit, earthiness and an edge of tar should be on display across all levels of quality. A string of exceptional vintages to start this century have pushed prices to sometimes dizzying heights. However, the opportunity to experience a top bottling from an exceptional vintage, perfected with proper cellaring, offers the potential epiphany of any wine enthusiast's lifetime.

MAJOR WHITE GRAPES:

Sauvignon Blanc

Semillon

Muscadelle

MAJOR RED GRAPES:

Cabernet Sauvignon

Merlot

Cabernet Franc

NOTEWORTHY SUB-REGIONS:

St. Estèphe

Pauillac

St. Julien

Margaux

St. Emilion

Pomerol

Graves

Pessac-Léognan

Sauternes

BORDEAUX

Bordeaux's red wines are the gold standard for Cabernet Sauvignon and Merlot, so I thought it appropriate for the Bordeaux Burger to be the yardstick by which all others should be judged. The recipe is modeled after the bistro classic, steak frites, but instead of beef, it is made with lamb, a specialty in Pauillac. Serving the burger on an English muffin with Stilton cheese is a tribute to the long-standing love that the British have had for Bordeaux's clarets.

RECOMMENDED COOKING METHOD: *Grill*   YIELDS: *4 servings*

BURGER INGREDIENTS:

1 ¼ lbs ground lamb

¼ cup finely chopped shallots

3 tbsp finely chopped parsley

2 tsp brine-preserved green peppercorns, drained and lightly chopped

1 tsp salt

SAUTÉED MUSHROOMS:

8 oz mushrooms, sliced

1 tbsp butter

1 tbsp Sherry vinegar

½ tsp fresh thyme leaves

¼ tsp salt

ASSEMBLE WITH:

4 English muffins, split and toasted

Stilton cheese

Lettuce

Sautéed mushrooms

SIDE DISH POMMES FRITES:

1 ½ lbs russet potatoes

Peanut oil for frying

1 tbsp finely chopped parsley

2 tsp kosher salt

TO PREPARE

1. **Prep potatoes** - Cut potatoes to desired thickness for French fries. Immediately submerge cut potatoes in a large bowl of cold water with 2 tablespoons white wine vinegar. Soak 15 minutes, then drain and cover with fresh cold water and vinegar.

In a separate bowl, combine parsley and salt.

2. **Combine burger ingredients** - Combine lamb, shallots, parsley, peppercorns and salt in a large mixing bowl and mix gently. Form burgers and set aside.

3. **Gather buns and toppings, set aside.**

COOK & SERVE

1. **Sauté mushrooms** - In a sauté pan set over high heat, add butter and mushrooms. Sauté until mushrooms start to caramelize. Add salt and Sherry vinegar, and continue cooking until moisture has evaporated. Add thyme and stir, and immediately remove from heat. Set aside.

2. **Blanch fries** - Fill a deep pot with about 4 inches of peanut oil, leaving at least 3 inches clearance from the top of the pot. Heat oil to 275°. Drain potatoes and pat dry with paper towels. Add fries to oil, and blanch until they just barely start to brown, about 6 minutes. Drain on a baking rack. Fries will be limp, but cooked through. The cooking process isn't done, so leave the oil where it is, but turn the heat down to low.

3. **Heat grill to 450°.**

4. **Grill burgers 3 to 4 minutes per side**, or until cooked to preferred doneness. Meanwhile, toast or grill English muffins.

5. **Finish cooking fries** - While burgers are resting, bring oil up to 375° and add fries. They will crisp up quickly, in about 90 seconds. Remove from oil and season with parsley salt immediately.

6. **Serve, topping burgers with lettuce, Stilton and sautéed mushrooms.**

BORDEAUX

TRADITIONAL PAIRINGS

Though it's not a steadfast rule, reds from Bordeaux's "Left Bank" communes are often composed of a high percentage of Cabernet Sauvignon, while "Right Bank" reds tend to be dominated by Merlot. Smaller amounts of Cabernet Franc, Malbec and Petit Verdot are often added to the blend for aromatic complexity and color.

	"Left Bank" AOCs:	*"Right Bank" AOCs:*
Red:	Pauillac	St. Emilion
	St. Estèphe	Pomerol
	St. Julien	Côtes de Blaye
	Margaux	Côtes du Bourg
	Graves	Fronsac
	Pessac-Léognan	Canon-Fronsac
	Médoc	Lalande-de-Pomerol
	Haut-Médoc	Bordeaux Supérieur
	Listrac	Entre-Deux-Mers
	Moulis	

ALTERNATE PAIRINGS

Super Tuscan reds, particularly those from Bolgheri on the Tuscan coastline

Reds from the Napa Valley in California

Top reds from Argentina

APPROPRIATE DESSERT WINE

Sauternes, arguably the greatest dessert wine in the world, made from grapes affected by *Botrytis cinerea*, also known as "Noble Rot". More affordable versions come from Barsac and Monbazillac.

BURGUNDY

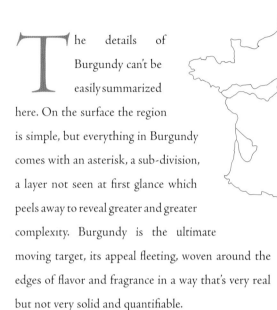

The details of Burgundy can't be easily summarized here. On the surface the region is simple, but everything in Burgundy comes with an asterisk, a sub-division, a layer not seen at first glance which peels away to reveal greater and greater complexity. Burgundy is the ultimate moving target, its appeal fleeting, woven around the edges of flavor and fragrance in a way that's very real but not very solid and quantifiable.

When "wine people" speak of Burgundy, the shorthand term is often meant to imply the Côte d'Or, or "golden slope" - the stretch of hills that run roughly north-south from Marsannay at the northern edge of the Côte de Nuits to Santenay, where the Côte de Beaune peters out into a patchwork of rolling hills, vines and farmland. But discontiguous Chablis in the cold north is a part of Burgundy, as are the Côte Chalonnaise and the Mâcon in the south. Even Gamay-filled Beaujolais in the far south (politically a part of the Rhône) belongs to viticultural Burgundy, though you'd be hard pressed to find a Burgophile who views it in quite the same light as its Pinot Noir-based brethren.

Long, historical explanations link these lands, but we are not writing a history of the Duchy of Burgundy. We are also not about to launch into a history of the Cistercians, a monastic order which contributed greatly to the landscape of modern Burgundy with their tireless mapping of the land into a deliciously fragmented blanket of Chardonnay and Pinot Noir vines.

So why are otherwise sane people willing to pay exponentially more for Chardonnay and Pinot Noir farmed in this cool corner of eastern France than from anywhere else in the world? To provoke an argument, and because it may be true, I say that Burgundy's best fields allow for as close to the creation of the true, pure expression of these noble varietals as a drinker can possibly experience. The converse is true as well: varietal character often cedes primacy to terroir in its best sites, particularly so when grapes are farmed by growers that keep intervention and ego to a minimum, to let their unique and evocative place take center stage. It takes courage to do less in the cellar, along with the wisdom to understand that nature may provide something latently more beautiful than man can craft.

BURGUNDY

Burgundy is great because it is not graspable. The characteristics its critics and imitators decry as flaws are often actually the virtues that make Burgundy desirable to its devotees. It is variable. Your experiences with Burgundy will rarely fall precisely in line with expectations. Far too often, the highly-anticipated pop of a cork can lead to disappointment, a fact that's hard to swallow (no pun intended) given the expense involved in developing an appreciation for Burgundy. To the outsider, the pathway to the real Burgundy is a minefield of the expensive and the banal, a frustrating way to waste a lot of cash on indifferent juice. Everyone in the region seems to make a dozen different wines from tiny slices of atrociously expensive land that trickled down to them in diminishing parcels via the Napoleonic code.

But the elusive great Burgundy epiphany is a spark that explodes into a lifelong obsession. The perfect, vanishing, yet eternal moment of pure enjoyment is, to many Burgundy drinkers, so much more valuable than reliable, repeatable experiences. This hits squarely at the center of human nature: we crave the challenge of grasping something ephemeral. Burgundy will remain the benchmark until – if? – another region can plausibly claim to bring forth from its soil so many different facets of the same grape, so much heterogeneous charm.

Enjoyment of Burgundy is often described as being the most sensual, ethereal form of wine enjoyment. But I think the opposite is also true; Burgundy exerts gravitational force on people unhappy with the black-and-white. It rewards those who desire an understanding of how nature speaks to us through wine, of why the secondary and tertiary notes keep changing, of why the margins of Burgundian character are so much more laden with expression than Chardonnay and Pinot Noir from elsewhere. There's a fortune to be spent and lifetime's worth of hairs to be split in attempting to answer these questions about Burgundy. We'd better get started…

MAJOR WHITE GRAPES:

Chardonnay

MAJOR RED GRAPES:

Pinot Noir

Gamay

NOTEWORTHY SUB-REGIONS:

Côte de Nuits

Côte de Beaune

Chablis

Côte Chalonnaise

Mâconnais

Beaujolais

BURGUNDY

Burgundy, one of the world's gastronomic capitals, has no shortage of incredible ingredients that could be used to create a sensational burger. Chicken from Bresse, mustard from Dijon, onions and mushrooms are all represented in this recipe, which is loosely modeled after Coq au Vin. The Burgundy Burger is equally suited to all the legendary whites and reds of Burgundy, so why not enjoy it with a glass each of Montrachet and Richebourg?

RECOMMENDED COOKING METHOD: *Cast Iron Pan*　YIELDS: *4 servings*

BURGER INGREDIENTS:

1¼ lbs ground chicken, preferably dark meat

½ cup finely chopped button mushrooms

2 tsp fresh thyme leaves

1 tbsp tomato paste

1 tsp celery salt

½ tsp ground black pepper

Breadcrumbs as needed

ASSEMBLE WITH:

4 burger buns, split

4 – 8 slices bacon

Onion slices

1 medium carrot, sliced into strips

Dijon mustard

SIDE DISH OVEN ROASTED PORTOBELLO CAPS:

4 large portobello mushrooms caps

½ tsp ground bay leaf or four whole bay leaves

2 tbsp finely chopped parsley

2 cloves minced garlic

½ tsp salt

3 tbsp butter, melted

TO PREPARE

1. **Prep portobello caps for side dish** - Remove mushroom stem, if still attached. Brush or rinse off any dirt on mushroom caps. Combine melted butter with ground bay leaf (see step 1 of cook & serve below if using whole bay leaves), chopped parsley, minced garlic and salt. Stir and set aside.

2. **Combine burger ingredients** - Gently mix chicken, button mushrooms, thyme leaves, tomato paste, celery salt and black pepper. Add breadcrumbs as necessary until you can form burgers without the mixture sticking to your hand too much. Form burgers and set aside.

3. **Gather buns and toppings, set aside.**

To make carrot strips of proper, even thickness: Rinse and peel the carrot, and trim the ends. Cut the carrot in half length-wise, and place on a cutting board, cut side up. Using a vegetable peeler, press down firmly and carefully peel down the flat side of the carrot to create about 12 thin strips.

COOK & SERVE

1. **Roast mushroom caps** - Preheat oven to 375°. Place the mushroom caps gill side up on a baking sheet. If using whole bay leaves instead of ground, place 1 leaf on each mushroom cap. Spread the butter-parsley-garlic mixture over the gills of the mushrooms. Roast 25-30 minutes. Remove bay leaves prior to serving.

2. **Cook bacon** - Cook 1 to 2 slices per burger in a large sauté pan.

3. Preheat a large cast iron pan over a 375° grill or on a stovetop burner set to medium-high heat. Drizzle the pan with vegetable oil just before adding burgers.

4. Cook burgers about 4 minutes per side, or until cooked to preferred doneness.

5. Serve, topping burgers with sliced onion, carrot strips, bacon and Dijon mustard.

TRADITIONAL PAIRINGS

With very few exceptions, white Burgundy is made from Chardonnay, while the reds are crafted from Pinot Noir. The most notable exception is in Beaujolais, where the reds are composed of the Gamay grape.

Space limitations prohibit an extensive inventory of the wine-producing villages of Burgundy, so below (where applicable) I have listed the AOCs you are most likely to encounter at a good wine shop.

Sparkling: Crémant de Bourgogne, made from Chardonnay, Aligoté, Pinot Blanc and Pinot Noir

White: Frequently encountered AOCs: Chablis, Meursault, Puligny-Montrachet, Chassagne-Montrachet, Pouilly-Fuissé, St. Véran, Viré-Clessé, Rully, Bourgogne blanc and various everyday whites from the Mâconnais, Côte Chalonnaise and Beaujolais

Red: Frequently encountered AOCs: Gevrey-Chambertin, Morey-St-Denis, Chambolle-Musigny, Vougeot, Vosne-Romanée, Nuits-St-George, Volnay, Pommard, Aloxe-Corton, Beaune, Savigny-lès-Beaune, Bourgogne rouge and Beaujolais

ALTERNATE PAIRINGS

Chardonnay and Pinot Noir from California, Oregon, New Zealand or Australia

Barolo and Barbaresco from Piedmont, Italy

Champagne

APPROPRIATE DESSERT WINE

Sélection de Grains Nobles from nearby Alsace, France

RHÔNE

The Rhône River begins high in the Swiss Alps and twists westward through France until it turns sharply south at the city of Lyon. This is where the winegrowing area of the Northern Rhône begins. Appellations of the Northern Rhône are stacked north to south along the river, unlike the Southern Rhône where they sprawl out into the more arable landscape. From Lyon, the river flows south for 230 miles until it empties into the Mediterranean Sea west of Marseille.

Le Mistral, the constant, cool wind that blows down the valley from the Alps, is a key contributor to the terroir of the Rhône, and the wines would be very different without it. It aids farmers by tempering the effects of the sun's scorching heat. This allows the grapes to retain acidity, which is essential to achieving balance in the finished wine. At harvest time the wind acts as a giant fan and keeps the grapes free of moisture that can cause mold. However, the wind can be so strong at times that vines must be pruned low to the ground to protect them from damage.

Dividing Rhône wines between north and south makes good sense, as there are vast differences between the two areas in landscape, soil, climate, and grape varieties. If the river did not provide a geographic connection, the Northern Rhône and the Southern Rhône would surely be seen as two separate wine regions. Around Lyon in the north, vines cling to granite and search for the sun amid oak forests and high-terraced cliffs, whereas near Avignon in the south, vines thrive amongst olive trees and herbal scrub on relatively flat land with plenty of sunshine.

The Northern Rhône's singular red grape is Syrah, which is at its worldwide best when grown on the steep vineyard sites of Hermitage. The appellation is a mere 300 acres on the top of a hill, making production minuscule and prices very high. Côte-Rôtie produces small amounts of Syrah that can be of stunning quality. The name literally means "roasted hillside" and refers to the vines clinging to the hillsides to catch the sun. The two most famous vineyard sites in Côte-Rôtie are Côte Brune and Côte Blonde. Legend has it that the slopes were named for the two daughters of a wealthy lord, one brunette and one blond. Wines from Côte Blonde are known to be lighter and more perfumed, while the Côte Brune are described as weightier and more tannic. Condrieu is the top-notch source for the floral, peachy Viognier grape. Elsewhere in the Northern Rhône you'll find varying amounts of Syrah, Viognier, Marsanne and Roussanne growing in the St. Joseph, Cornas and Crozes-Hermitage appellations.

The Southern Rhône is flatter than its counterpart, and its vintners specialize in blended wines. Reds are dominated by Grenache, which is often blended with Mourvèdre and Syrah, resulting in lighter, berry-scented wine. The climate of the south is Mediterranean, with hot dry summers. The ground below the low, bushy vines is often covered in stones, known as *galets*, which retain heat during the day and help to produce the ripe and juicy character of Southern Rhône wines.

Châteauneuf-du-Pape, which permits the blending of up to thirteen red and white grapes, is the most significant appellation in the south for two reasons: they produce more wine than all the northern appellations combined, and their wines are well-known and prized among collectors. The reds can be characterized as wild, with earthy, gamy flavors. White Châteauneuf-du-Pape shows aromas of honeysuckle and white flowers. Gigondas is known for rustic red and rosé made mostly from Grenache with some Syrah or Mourvèdre. Several excellent producers in Beaumes-de-Venise produce a sweet fortified white wine made from the floral and exotic Muscat grape.

Roughly 75 percent of all Rhône wine is labeled as Côtes du Rhône, of which the vast majority comes from the Southern Rhône. There are 96 villages that can add the word "Villages" to their label, which is supposed to indicate a step up in quality, but this is not always the case. Because of the size of the territory and variance of soil that these grapes can be grown in, Côtes du Rhône wines range from humble quaffing wines to serious efforts that can emulate a decent Châteauneuf-du-Pape, with a thousand shades in between. As such, it pays to buy from a respected producer.

MAJOR WHITE GRAPES:

Viognier

Roussanne

Marsanne

MAJOR RED GRAPES:

Grenache

Syrah

Mourvèdre

NOTEWORTHY SUB-REGIONS:

Hermitage

Crozes-Hermitage

Côte·Rôtie

St. Joseph

Condrieu

Châteauneuf-du-Pape

Gigondas

Tavel

If the Loire Valley is the "Garden of France" then the Rhône Valley should be known as the "Orchard of France". Some of the country's finest fruits come from the Rhône Valley, particularly peaches, cherries, nectarines, plums, strawberries and raspberries. The grapes aren't bad either. This bounty, combined with the Rhône's proximity to Lyon's famous bouchons, creates an enviable epicenter for good eating. The Rhône Burger is created with a minimalist approach, and is tailored to both the reds and whites of the region.

RECOMMENDED COOKING METHOD: *Grill*   YIELDS: *4 servings*

BURGER INGREDIENTS:

1 ½ lbs ground pork

½ tsp ground white pepper

2 tbsp finely chopped parsley

1 tsp salt

ASSEMBLE WITH:

4 burger buns, split

1 peach, sliced and sautéed or grilled

Beaufort, Comté or Gruyère cheese slices

Frisée lettuce

SIDE DISH FRISÉE SALAD WITH RASPBERRY VINAIGRETTE:

1 small head / 4 cups frisée lettuce

1 plum, cut into 8 slices

½ cup table grapes, sliced

¼ cup crushed walnuts

Sprinkle of sea salt

RASPBERRY VINAIGRETTE:

½ cup fresh raspberries

¼ cup olive oil

3 tbsp white wine vinegar

1 tbsp honey

Salt and pepper to taste

TO PREPARE

1. **Make raspberry vinaigrette** - Purée raspberries in a food processor, then, using a fine-mesh sieve to remove the seeds, strain into a bowl. Whisk in olive oil, white wine vinegar and honey. Season with salt and pepper to taste.

2. **Combine burger ingredients** - Gently mix pork, white pepper, parsley and salt in a large mixing bowl. Form patties and set aside.

3. **Gather buns and toppings, set aside.**

COOK & SERVE

1. **Cook peaches** - Slice peaches about ⅛-inch thick. Sauté peach slices in a splash of olive oil, or brush with oil and grill until just barely soft and lightly caramelized.

2. **Assemble salad** - Top lettuce with sliced plum, grapes, crushed walnuts and a light sprinkle of sea salt. Dress with raspberry vinaigrette just before serving.

3. **Heat grill to 375°.**

4. **Grill burgers 3 to 4 minutes per side, or until cooked to preferred doneness. Add Beaufort, Comté or Gruyère during final minute of cooking.**

5. **Serve, topping burgers with peaches and frisée lettuce.**

RHÔNE

TRADITIONAL PAIRINGS

	Noteworthy AOCs:	*Grape(s):*
White:	Condrieu	Viognier
	Hermitage and St. Joseph	Marsanne, Roussanne
	Châteauneuf-du-Pape	Roussanne, Grenache Blanc, Bourboulenc, Clairette
	Côtes du Rhône	Grenache Blanc, Marsanne, Roussanne, Clairette, Bourboulenc
Rosé:	Tavel	Grenache
Red:	Hermitage, Cote-Rôtie, Crozes-Hermitage and St. Joseph	Syrah
	Châteauneuf-du-Pape and Gigondas	Grenache, Syrah, Mourvèdre
	Côtes du Rhône	Grenache, Syrah, Carignan
	Costières de Nîmes	Grenache, Syrah, Carignan, Cinsault, Mourvèdre

---

ALTERNATE PAIRINGS

Rhône varietals from California's Central Coast, Sonoma and Napa

Grenache, Syrah and Viognier from Australia

Wines from neighboring Languedoc-Roussillon

APPROPRIATE DESSERT WINE

Vin de Paille, made from grapes dried on straw mats, and Muscat de Beaumes de Venise.

LANGUEDOC-ROUSSILLON

Warm, arid and sunny, the Languedoc-Roussillon is a wide swath of land along the southern coast of France, stretching from Spain to the Rhône River at Arles. There are similarities between this region and its neighbors to the east - Provence and the Southern Rhône. This is an easy place to grow grapes, and there are many, many people doing so, both winemakers as well as growers selling off their harvest. The region's surrounding hills protect it from the extremes of the Mediterranean and Atlantic climates, and it enjoys a microclimate particularly suitable for making quality wine. Much of the cultivation is on a flat plain facing the Mediterranean, but the best vineyards are higher up on the cooler plateaus and foothills of the Pyrenees Mountains. The landscape is full of low bushes and wild herbs called *garrigue*, the scrubland growth reflected in the wines in the form of earthy, herbal aromas of lavender, rosemary and thyme.

The Languedoc's coastline along the Mediterranean Sea is a stretch of about 120 miles, extending inland about 50 miles at the most. The growing areas of this region are divided into a number of appellations, the most famous being Côteaux du Languedoc, Corbières,

Minervois , Pic-St-Loup and St-Chinian, all of which are known for red wines at great bargain prices.

Limoux makes a delicious sparkling wine from the native Mauzac grape called Blanquette de Limoux. As the story goes, this was the world's first sparkling wine. Dating back to the 1500s, the monks of the Benedictine Abbey of Saint-Hilaire in the Languedoc were producing an unusual white wine in their cellars. Inside its glass flask, fitted with a cork top - very rare for wines at this time - it acquired a natural sparkle. This occurred well over a century before another Benedictine, Dom Pierre Pérignon, perfected the more familiar fizzy wine that caught the world's attention as Champagne.

As one of France's most prolific wine regions, the Languedoc has experienced the pitfalls of overproduction, low quality and subsequent sinking value. Despite this, since the end of the 1990s standards and reputation have begun to ascend. One problem affecting quality is its extremely fertile soil and easy growing conditions, leading to high yields of grapes of unremarkable quality. To make better wine with more complexity and longevity, a winegrower must choose to reduce yields and farm in poorer soil sites, forcing the vines to send roots deep into the soil.

The Roussillon is a very different place than the Languedoc. Culturally, the Roussillon is tied to Spanish Catalonia, having been a part of this region and governed by Spain until the late seventeenth century. Its climate is extreme, even by Mediterranean standards, and it's known for having one of the warmest, driest and longest growing seasons in France. It also stands apart from the Languedoc in its wine industry. The Roussillon is known for producing 90 percent of France's Vins Doux Naturels, a sweet fortified wine typically crafted from very ripe grapes whose fermentation is halted before absolute completion with the addition of a neutral spirit. The most famous of these is the red Banyuls, which comes from the southwestern-most corner of France's coastline, bordering Spain in the foothills of the Pyrenees Mountains where they disappear into the Mediterranean Sea. These low hills contain scrubby-looking vines of Grenache, many with decades of age that yield very small amounts of fruit. Dry wines from the Roussillon are most commonly labeled as Côtes du Roussillon, and are often a blend of Carignan, Syrah, Mourvèdre and Grenache. White wines are typically made from Grenache Blanc, Marsanne, Roussane, Vermentino and Macabeo.

With such a vast amount of vineyard space, wines from the Languedoc-Roussillon are understandably a mixed bag in terms of quality. Much of what is imported to the US is of respectable quality, with the occasional standout bottling. In most cases the wines are ideally suited to the rustic cuisine of the area, which features game birds, pork, lamb and plenty of seafood.

MAJOR WHITE GRAPES:

Macabeo

Grenache Blanc

Bourboulenc

Picpoul

MAJOR RED GRAPES:

Carignan

Syrah

Grenache

Mourvèdre

NOTEWORTHY SUB-REGIONS:

Corbières

Minervois

Coteaux du Languedoc

Pic-St-Loup

Costières de Nîmes

St-Chinian

Cassoulet, the inspiration for this recipe, is country cooking at its finest. It is a specialty in the town of Castelnaudary in the Languedoc, and throughout southern France. Cassoulet is essentially a white bean stew, augmented with varying amounts of fresh pork, ham, bacon, sausage, duck, goose and/or lamb. Creating the genuine article can take days, but this loving homage simplifies the process and minimizes the time commitment. The white bean spread adds in a few indispensible Languedoc foodstuffs not included in a traditional Cassoulet.

RECOMMENDED COOKING METHOD: **Grill**   YIELDS: **4 servings**

BURGER INGREDIENTS:

¾ lb finely chopped duck (two duck breasts, with skin and fat)

¾ lb ground pork

2 tsp fresh thyme leaves

2 tbsp tomato paste

½ tsp ground black pepper

1 tsp salt

WHITE BEAN AND OLIVE PURÉE:

¼ cup olive oil, more as needed

1 15-oz can white beans (cannellini or great northern), drained and rinsed

2 cloves crushed garlic

1 tsp ground fennel

½ cup whole pitted black olives

2 tbsp mayonnaise

½ tsp salt

¼ tsp ground black pepper

ASSEMBLE WITH:

4 burger buns, split

4 – 8 slices bacon

Onion slices

White bean and olive purée

SIDE DISH STUFFED TOMATOES:

4 medium-large tomatoes

¼ cup lightly chopped black olives

½ cup crumbled goat cheese

1 cup rice (makes 1 ½ cups cooked)

¼ cup breadcrumbs

2 cloves minced garlic

2 tsp finely chopped rosemary

1 tsp salt

½ tsp ground black pepper

¼ cup olive oil, plus more for drizzling

TO PREPARE

1. **Make white bean and olive purée** - Heat olive oil in a sauté pan over medium-high heat, and add white beans, garlic and fennel. Sauté 3 to 5 minutes, or until beans are lightly browned. Transfer to a small food processor and add black olives, mayonnaise and salt. Pulse until smooth, drizzling in olive oil as needed to achieve desired texture. Transfer to a small bowl and set aside.

2. **Prep tomatoes** - Boil rice in 1 ½ cups water until cooked through, approximately 20 minutes, then remove from heat. Meanwhile, cut the top off of each tomato and discard. Using a spoon, hollow out the inside of the tomato. In a mixing bowl, combine rice, chopped olives, goat cheese crumbles, breadcrumbs, garlic, chopped rosemary, olive oil, salt and pepper. Scoop the mixture into the hollowed-out tomatoes and drizzle with olive oil.

3. **Combine burger ingredients** - Cut duck breasts into 1-inch pieces and place in food processor. Pulse until no large chunks remain. Transfer to a mixing bowl and combine with ground pork, thyme leaves, tomato paste, pepper and salt. Mix gently, form burgers and set aside.

4. **Gather buns and toppings, set aside.**

COOK & SERVE

1. **Cook bacon** - Cook 1 to 2 slices per burger in large sauté pan.

2. **Roast tomatoes** - Preheat oven to 400°. Place tomatoes on a baking sheet and roast 20 minutes.

3. **Heat grill to 375°.**

4. **Grill burgers 4 minutes per side, or until cooked to preferred doneness.**

5. **Serve, topping burgers with bacon, onion and white bean and olive purée.**

LANGUEDOC-ROUSSILLON

	Noteworthy AOCs:	*Grape(s):*
Rosé:	Numerous rosés come from the appellations listed below, and are composed primarily of Grenache, Syrah and Cinsault	
Red:	Corbières	Carignan, Grenache, Syrah, Mourvèdre, Cinsault
	Coteaux du Languedoc, Pic-St-Loup	Grenache, Syrah, Mourvèdre, Carignan, Cinsault
	Côtes du Roussillon	Carignan, Syrah, Mourvèdre, Grenache
	Many more reds, which may also include Cabernet Sauvignon, Merlot and Cabernet Franc	

ALTERNATE PAIRINGS

Reds from the Palette AOC in Provence

Grenache-based reds from Spain, California and Australia

Rustic reds from southern Italy

APPROPRIATE DESSERT WINE

Banyuls, a fortified Grenache from Roussillon

PROVENCE

Provence becons, both figuratively and in reality. If given a free plane ticket to anywhere in the world...St. Remy, here we come! Separating the experience of unhurried days in a Mediterranean paradise from the wines tasted in those happy hours requires a cold objectivity possessed by a tiny fragment of (probably emotionless and miserable) humanity. You get swept up in Provence, and the local rosé seems good, relevant, perfect even; clearly the only thing to drink on the tree-lined streets, red-tile-capped patios, or on picnics amidst olive trees and wild, aromatic scrublands. Provence is a wine country in a way that is remarkable among wine growing regions: wine simply *happens* during so many moments of life here. The cuisine, mindset and even landscape seem to spin outward from the flavor of this indispensable beverage.

Wisdom holds that away from Bandol, not a lot of exciting wine is made in Provence. This point of view really doesn't stand up under scrutiny. Sure, when you compare Provence to the neighboring Rhône, Provençal wine seems trifling. But is this really a fair, necessary or relevant comparison? Not every glass of wine needs to be a mind-blowing experience to create

happiness. Sometimes it's better to enhance than to overwhelm an otherwise perfect moment. What's more, the division between Provence and the Rhône is more political than cultural, the boundaries less cleanly drawn than wine books generally imply. Provence's heavy commercial reliance on rosé may seem a hindrance to some, but why? Oceans of innocuous pink wine are made and sold along the Côte d'Azur, to locals and to tourists exploring its sun-baked towns. But people love it, and it's certainly no worse than the *vin ordinaire* of any number of the more highly regarded French wine regions.

Nothing especially nervy, mineral or esoteric is likely to arise from the fields of Provence. The snob appeal of its wines may be low, but quality wine does exist in its cellars. In discussing any wine region, writers and critics generally remain focused on the small fraction of growers making exceptional, character-filled wine. And while that core group may be smaller in Provence than elsewhere, the wines these farmers craft are no less evocative. A perfectly framed, seamless and delicate rosé from the Côtes de Provence is a thing of beauty, a rare treat as enjoyable as a perfect flute of Champagne.

Often (but not always) the color is a dead giveaway. To the trained rosé-fiend's eye this particular hue of pink, somewhere between carnation, tangerine and salmon, is enough to make the admirer salivate. With a bouillabaisse, Niçoise salad, or even just an assortment of local olives and summer tomatoes, this type of rosé makes for a dream dinner.

There are other colors to Provence as well. The local reds do well, particularly when Syrah and Grenache are the main ingredients, and a surprising (and surprisingly successful) amount of Cabernet Sauvignon is present in the fields sandwiched between the Massif des Maures and the Mediterranean. Whites based on Rolle (Vermentino in Italy), Ugni Blanc (Trebbiano) and Clairette are a common component of the Provençal vinescape. These grapes can be made into memorable and refreshing wines when they are planted in cooler-climate vineyards. Typically these are higher-elevation sites, or vineyards in close proximity to the sea. But ultimately, it all comes down to the Mourvèdre, Grenache and Cinsault that go into the Provençal rosés which makes such a lasting impression during your time in this Mediterranean version of Eden.

MAJOR WHITE GRAPES:

Ugni Blanc

Clairette

Bourboulenc

Rolle

MAJOR RED GRAPES:

Mourvèdre

Grenache

Cinsault

Syrah

NOTEWORTHY SUB-REGIONS:

Côtes de Provence

Coteaux d'Aix-en-Provence

Bandol

Cassis

Palette

PROVENCE

The Provence Burger is an interpretation of the Niçoise specialty, Pan-bagnat, which uses clean, bright flavors to create the perfect partner for the area's beautiful dry rosés. Fresh tuna is accented with black olive and the ubiquitous herbes de Provence. The toppings are minimal, as we don't want to overshadow the delicate flavor of the tuna. Pistou, a Provençal condiment similar to pesto, adds a bright punch of flavor to both the burger and the side dish of roasted artichokes.

RECOMMENDED COOKING METHOD: *Non-stick sauté pan*   YIELDS: *4 servings*

BURGER INGREDIENTS:

1 ½ lbs finely chopped fresh tuna, skin removed

¼ cup finely chopped black olives

1 tsp fresh thyme leaves

1 tsp dried lavender

½ tsp ground rosemary

¼ tsp ground fennel seed

¼ tsp dried oregano

1 tsp anchovy paste

1 tsp salt

PISTOU (FOR BURGERS AND ARTICHOKES):

½ cup olive oil

1 cup fresh basil

1 clove garlic

½ tsp salt

ASSEMBLE WITH:

4 burger buns, split

Pistou

Tomato slices

Frisée lettuce

SIDE DISH **BAKED ARTICHOKES WITH PISTOU:**

4 artichokes

½ tsp dried oregano

½ tsp salt

Olive oil

Pepper, to taste

TO PREPARE

1. **Make pistou** - Combine basil and garlic in a small food processor and pulse until basil is finely chopped. Add olive oil and salt and purée until smooth. Pour into serving bowl and set aside.

2. **Combine burger ingredients** - Cut tuna into 1-inch cubes and place in small food processor. Pulse until there are no longer any large chunks, but avoid grinding the tuna to a paste. Transfer to a mixing bowl and combine with black olives, all the herbs, anchovy paste and salt. Mix gently. Form burgers and refrigerate until you are ready to cook.

3. **Prep artichokes** - Use a pair of scissors to cut the sharp points off of the leaves of 4 artichokes. Cut artichokes in half, lengthwise. Using a paring knife, cut into the heart of the artichoke, just underneath the layer of fuzz, and scrape out the fuzz and inner leaves to reveal the clean heart of the artichoke. Since the artichokes will be sautéed and roasted there is no reason to worry about the oxidation that will occur.

4. **Gather buns and toppings, set aside.**

COOK & SERVE

1. **Cook artichokes** - Preheat oven to 375°. Bring a large pot of salted water to a boil. Add artichokes and par boil 10 minutes. Remove and drain on paper towels. Heat a large sauté pan to medium-high with 1 tablespoon of oil. Sauté artichokes cut side down, until lightly browned. Transfer artichokes to a baking sheet cut side up. Sprinkle with dried oregano, salt and pepper, and roast for 25-30 minutes.

2. **Cook burgers** - Using the same large sauté pan, heat 1 tablespoon of olive oil on medium-high. Once oil is heated, add burgers and sauté about 3 minutes per side or until tuna is cooked to preferred doneness. I like mine on the rare side, but for a more fully-cooked burger, place a lid on the sauté pan and cook an additional 2 to 3 minutes.

3. **Serve, topping burgers with tomato, frisée lettuce and a spoonful of the pistou. Serve a side of the remaining pistou with the baked artichokes.**

PROVENCE

Artichokes

	Noteworthy AOCs:	*Grape(s):*
White:	Coteaux d'Aix-en-Provence	Bourboulenc, Clairette, Grenache Blanc
	Cassis	Clairette, Marsanne, Ugni Blanc, Sauvignon Blanc
Rosé:	Côtes de Provence	Carignan, Cinsault, Grenache, Mourvèdre, Tibouren
	Coteaux d'Aix-en-Provence	Grenache, Cinsault, Mourvèdre
	Bandol	Mourvèdre, Grenache, Cinsault

ALTERNATE PAIRINGS

Other great dry rosés from around the world:

Tavel and others from France's Rhône Valley

Rosado from Rioja and elsewhere in Spain

Rosato from Italy, particularly those made from the Lagrein grape in Alto Adige

Numerous others from the U.S., Australia, South America, Austria and Portugal

---

APPROPRIATE DESSERT WINE

Rivesaltes, from Languedoc-Roussillon

ITALY

Due to its diverse climate, varied topography and well over one thousand different grape varieties, Italy defies simple descriptions and generalizations. The country is essentially one giant vineyard; wine is made in all twenty regions, ranging in quality from awe-inspiring, to everyday quaffers, to those best left for distillation. Noteworthy wines come from every region, but not every region is regarded as required reading (or drinking, rather) for the everyday enjoyment of Italy's broad offerings. For a master class on Italian wine, look no further than *Vino Italiano: The Regional Wines of Italy* (Bastianich/Lynch; Clarkson Potter Publishers), the bible for Italian wine.

Like France's AOC system, Italy's Denominazione di Origine Controllata, or DOC, was created to designate a place of origin and guarantee that only certain grape varieties make it into the bottle. Unfortunately, it has not been as successful as its French counterpart, and did little to inspire winemakers to make the best wine possible. Permissible yields-per-acre were atrociously high and experimentation with superior grape varieties came at the expense of DOC status. The creation of the DOCG (which appends "e Garantita," or "and guaranteed") implies, and in most cases delivers, a greater level of quality, with stricter standards than DOC qualification.

Even with the creation of the DOCG, little was being done to push producers to make the best wine they could. Ambitious winemakers, at the expense of a more sellable product, chose to forego DOC and DOCG status in exchange for the lowly Vino da Tavola, which allowed them to make wine the way they saw fit. The trend became so commonplace that in 1992 a new category called Indicazione Geografica Tipica, or IGT, was created as a way of indicating a place of origin, while not granting DOC status.

There are many gray areas and ambiguities when it comes to Italian wine, but deciphering the place of origin and the grape(s) that go into making a particular wine is arguably the biggest stumbling block in understanding Italian wine. It can be difficult to determine whether the label is indicating the name of a grape, a place of origin, both or neither. Look at the "pairings" section at the end of each recipe for key DOCs and the grapes that are grown within their boundaries.

PIEDMONT

One of Europe's finest winegrowing regions, Piedmont is nestled within the fog-covered Langhe and Monferrato hills, and is centered around the historic town of Alba. The area is nearly encircled by the Alps and Appenine Mountains, hence the name *Piemonte*, meaning "at the foot of the mountain." The Mediterranean Sea lies to the south, separated from Piedmont by the region of Liguria, with its narrow coastline dotted with fishing villages and vineyards yielding their own respectable wines.

Formerly a part of France's Kingdom of Savoy, Piedmont's culture has for centuries been influenced by French style and taste, particularly in its cuisine and viticulture. During those years and throughout the Enlightenment of Europe, Piedmont was protected and prosperous, in stark contrast to the rest of the Italian peninsula. The resulting advancement of Piedmont's wine industry made it Italy's most stable and evolved winegrowing region, bolstered by the identification of the best vineyard sites for native grape varieties, greater understanding of the science of fermentation and superior skills in the aging of their wines.

Piedmont's reputation is built largely on its two most important wines, Barolo and Barbaresco. Named for the towns from which they hail, both wines are crafted exclusively from the Nebbiolo grape and may be counted among the best that the world has to offer. Stylistic differences exist between – and within – Barolo and Barbaresco. Barolo is generally the more structured of the two wines, while Barbaresco features softer, more perfumed elegance. Traditionalists in each town ferment their wines in large, old wooden casks and allow the juice to soak with the grape skins for a period of up to two months, imparting sturdy tannins that require significant cellaring before the wine can express all of its charm. More modern-minded producers emphasize shorter maceration times, followed by aging in smaller, new oak barrels. These wines are smooth and approachable at a far younger age, comparatively speaking, and represent a more extroverted side of Nebbiolo.

As in France's Burgundy region, the grapes that go into Barolo and Barbaresco are sourced from small parcels of meticulously tended land that are divided among numerous growers. While no Grand Cru- or Premier Cru-like classification exists in Piedmont, mere mention of a top vineyard site such as Brunate, Monprivato or Asili will get a Piedmont enthusiast's mouth watering.

Incredible as they are, Barolo and Barbaresco represent just a portion of the complete Piedmont wine experience. Varietally-labeled Barbera, Dolcetto and straightforward renditions of Nebbiolo are often enjoyable, occasionally inspiring, more affordable alternatives for everyday enjoyment. They range from light, berry-scented quaffers to deep, dark, structured wines that can give entry-level Barolo and Barbaresco a run for their money.

Piedmont is first and foremost a red wine region, but because the quality of viticulture throughout the area is so universally high, the whites continue to gain recognition. Gavi, made from the Cortese grape, is the most well known of Piedmont's whites, while the floral Arneis grape is gaining ground among Italy's finest *biancos*. Not to be underestimated, sweet and fizzy Moscato d'Asti is equally enjoyable as an introduction to a meal as at its conclusion. If that weren't enough, the country's best *Metodo Classico* sparkling wines are made (sometimes by Piemontese producers) in neighboring Lombardy, in the Franciacorta DOCG.

With all this top-notch viticulture, you'd be right to assume that there's equally fantastic food. An amazing selection of agricultural products, including highly prized fruits, vegetables, grains, hazelnuts and chestnuts are staples of the Piemontese kitchen. Butter and cream are also more common here than in most other parts of Italy, as cows can thrive where olive trees cannot. The animals that graze throughout Piedmont's alpine pastures yield some of Italy's best meats and a variety of cheeses; perfect antipasti to accompany a thorough sampling of the area's wines. When the crisp autumn weather descends it's foraging time for the area's most famous ingredient: the white truffle of Alba. This bounty, combined with some of the finest wines in the world, forms the enviable culinary experience of the Piedmont.

MAJOR WHITE GRAPES:

Arneis

Cortese

Moscato

MAJOR RED GRAPES:

Nebbiolo

Barbera

Dolcetto

Brachetto

NOTEWORTHY SUB-REGIONS:

Barolo

Barbaresco

Asti

Alba

Ghemme

Gattinara

Roero

Gavi

Acqui

Langhe

PIEDMONT

Home to the Slow Food organization, Piedmont boasts a hearty, robust cuisine well suited to the cold climate of the Alps, which pairs perfectly with the earthy, sturdy reds of the region. Piedmont's agricultural treasure is the elusive white truffle of Alba. While I don't suggest grating a $1,200-per-pound tuber into your burger, a dash of truffle oil and a handful of perfectly sautéed porcini on top of this succulent lamb burger will do the trick nicely, particularly when paired with a properly matured Barolo or Barbaresco.

RECOMMENDED COOKING METHOD: *Grill*   YIELDS: *4 servings*

BURGER INGREDIENTS:

1 ½ lbs ground lamb

⅓ cup finely chopped shallot

2 tbsp finely chopped rosemary

1 tbsp fresh thyme leaves

1 tbsp ground coriander seed

1 tsp truffle oil

1 tsp salt

MUSHROOMS

(FOR BURGERS AND POLENTA):

8 oz fresh porcini mushrooms or 2 oz dried

2 tbsp butter

1 tbsp finely chopped rosemary

½ tsp salt

ASSEMBLE WITH:

4 burger buns, split

Fontina cheese slices

Sautéed porcini mushrooms

Lettuce

SIDE DISH POLENTA WITH MUSHROOMS:

3 cups veal or chicken stock

1 tbsp butter

1 cup polenta

¼ cup heavy cream

1 cup grated Fontina cheese

Water, as needed

Salt and pepper, to taste

Half of the sautéed porcini

TO PREPARE

1. **Prep porcini mushrooms** - If using dehydrated mushrooms, reconstitute by soaking in warm water for 30 minutes. Chop the rosemary and set aside.

2. **Combine burger ingredients** - In a large mixing bowl, gently mix lamb, shallot, rosemary, thyme, coriander, truffle oil and salt. Form burgers and set aside.

3. **Gather buns and toppings, set aside.**

COOK & SERVE

1. **Sauté mushrooms** - Melt butter in a sauté pan over medium-high heat. Add mushrooms and sauté until lightly browned. Add salt, and continue cooking for 1 minute. Add rosemary for the final 30 seconds of cooking. Set aside.

2. **Cook polenta** - Bring veal stock, butter, and a pinch of salt to a boil. Very slowly add the polenta, stirring constantly. Once all the polenta is in, reduce heat to low and keep stirring. Once all the stock has been absorbed, add the heavy cream and Fontina and continue stirring. Taste for seasoning and doneness. Add water ¼ cup at a time if needed to fully soften the polenta. When cooked through, add sautéed porcini mushrooms. Assuming you're not using instant polenta (you're not, right?), cooking time will be around 45 minutes. Remove from heat. If it cools too much before serving, warm the polenta over medium heat while burgers rest.

3. **Heat grill to 450°.**

4. **Grill burgers about 3 to 4 minutes per side, or until cooked to preferred doneness. Add Fontina during final minute of cooking.**

5. **Serve, topping burgers with lettuce and sautéed porcini.**

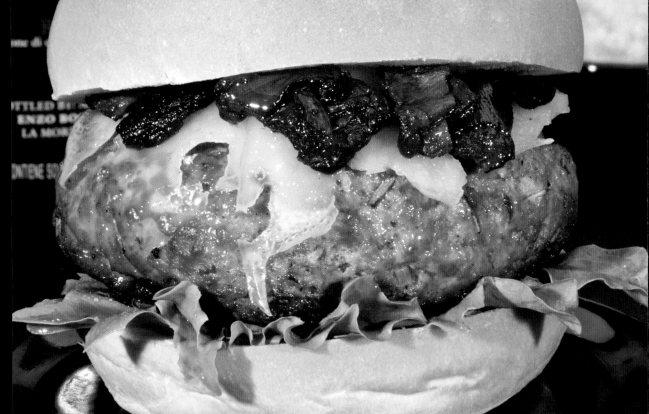

TRADITIONAL PAIRINGS

	Noteworthy DOC(G)s:	*Grape(s):*
Red:	Barolo, Barbaresco, Ghemme, Gattinara	Nebbiolo
	Barbera d'Asti, Barbera d'Alba	Barbera
	Dolcetto d'Asti, Dolcetto d'Alba, Dolcetto di Dogliani	Dolcetto
	Langhe rosso (red blend)	Nebbiolo, Barbera, Dolcetto, Bonarda, Grignolino, Freisa

Vino da Tavola reds composed of indigenous varietals, as well as Cabernet Sauvignon, Cabernet Franc, Syrah and Merlot

---

ALTERNATE PAIRINGS

Reds from neighboring Lombardy and Val d'Aosta regions

Red Burgundy

Red Bordeaux with 10+ years of age

APPROPRIATE DESSERT WINE

Moscato d'Asti

Brachetto d'Acqui

VENETO

Located in the western part of the Veneto, Verona seems a formal city at first. Grey skies hang over weathered stone buildings, lining the streets that wend toward the pedestrian heart of town and its imposing coliseum. Agriculture begins almost immediately on the outskirts of the city, but the land is flat, in places drab, in others marred by industry. The valleys running north from Verona toward the Alps and Austria break up this monotony and offer reason for optimism. The vast majority of the Veneto's prime viticultural zones surround Verona, making it an ideal jumping-off point for visiting the region's top estates.

Wines of Valpolicella present a wealth of diversity from a simple palate of ingredients. Corvina, Rondinella and Molinara are the main components of its most prominent red wines. Basic Valpolicella is fragrant, soft and dominated by red berry fruit aromas, though others are concentrated and dark, extracted, low in acidity and marked by new oak. One of Italy's most memorable wines, and certainly Valpolicella's finest, Amarone is made using those same grapes. With the harvest spread out on straw mats, open barn and attic doors expose slumbering grapes to the constant breeze blowing south from the Alps and through the valleys surrounding Verona, partially drying them. Amarone is a memorable wine, big and primary and often Port-like in concentration, particularly when young. Low yields, intensive labor and significant aging translate to uniformly high prices, particularly for the unctuous, sweet version known as Recioto. Beware of cheap Amarone - you are being cheated by anyone selling such an improbable item.

Somewhere between Valpolicella and Amarone, you'll find wines labeled as Ripasso (literally "re-passed") which attain additional richness and complexity as regular Valpolicella mingles with the grape skins left over from Amarone production. Luckily for us, a good Ripasso hints at Amarone's greatness at a fraction of the cost. All of these reds make excellent companions to the meat-heavy cuisine of the Veneto. Even if you aren't eating horse (an omnipresent local entrée), you will be served a wallop of delicious starches, dairy and meat. Bring your appetite.

To the east, Prosecco from Conegliano and Valdobbiadene and Garganega from Soave offer delicious refreshment. However, both wines share a common problem: cheap, slap-dash – if not outright fraudulent – versions of wine bearing their name sit on millions of store shelves and dinner tables around the globe, sullying the reputations of wines that deserve to be considered as uniquely Italian food products. Most Americans who consumed Soave in recent decades knew it simply as large-scale, low-character wine found on the bottom shelf of their local grocery store. Now, far more deserving examples are easy to find at your favorite quality-minded wine merchant. In its authentic form, Prosecco is a vibrant first-course sparkler that lifts light cuisine and animates conversation. Most Prosecco is light quaffing wine, but the best examples begin their life in the Cartizze hills, perfectly suited to this late-ripening grape.

The Veneto is dotted with other interesting diversions. Bardolino is a juicy change of pace from Valpolicella. The region's wines are terrific lunch time reds, low enough in alcohol and tannin to sip midday before setting out into the beautiful lake country that surrounds this DOC. South of Verona, Bianco di Custoza is made. The wines of this area don't match the best from the Soave Classico region in texture or heady aromatics, but they are often minerally and pure, snappy whites that go great with simple preparations of trout from nearby Lake Garda.

MAJOR WHITE GRAPES:

Garganega

Trebbiano

Prosecco

MAJOR RED GRAPES:

Corvina

Rondinella

Molinara

Cabernet Sauvignon

Cabernet Franc

NOTEWORTHY SUB-REGIONS:

Valpolicella

Soave

Bardolino

Lugana
(shared with Lombardy)

VENETO

The Veneto is home to a diverse array of some of Italy's most enjoyable wines, from inexpensive sparkling Prosecco to the intense and alluring Amarone. My goal was to create a burger that would work well with all the reds and whites that the Veneto has to offer. While it would be perfectly appropriate to make this burger with chicken, beef or even horse meat (if you want to be as authentic as possible), veal pairs well with all of the Veneto's vinous contributions.

RECOMMENDED COOKING METHOD: *Grill*   YIELDS: *4 servings*

BURGER INGREDIENTS:

1 ½ lbs ground veal

1 cup coarsely grated Asiago cheese

1 tsp ginger powder

1 tsp salt

CHERRY RELISH:

1 cup veal stock

½ cup red wine

¼ cup red wine vinegar

½ cup lightly chopped dried cherries

1 cup diced celery

ASSEMBLE WITH:

4 burger buns, split

Lettuce

Cherry relish

4 – 8 slices pancetta (or bacon)

SIDE DISH RISI E BISI:

1 cup Arborio rice

½ cup peas (thawed, if frozen)

3 cups veal stock, or as needed

2 tbsp butter

2 tbsp lightly chopped parsley

1 cup coarsely grated Asiago cheese

Salt to taste

TO PREPARE

1. **Prep ingredients for cherry relish.**

2. **Combine burger ingredients** - Gently mix ground veal, grated Asiago, ginger powder and salt in a large mixing bowl. Form burgers and set aside.

3. **Gather buns and toppings, set aside.**

COOK & SERVE

1. **Make cherry relish** - In a small saucepan, simmer dried cherries in veal stock, red wine and vinegar. Cook until liquid has reduced to a light syrup consistency. Remove from heat.

2. **Cook risotto and peas (*risi e bisi*)** - Melt butter in a large skillet over medium-high heat. Add rice and stir for about 2 minutes. Add 2 cups of stock and continue stirring. As stock is absorbed, add more, ½ cup at a time. Stir often for about 20 minutes, until rice begins to soften and starch develops, creating the risotto's own sauce. When risotto reaches al dente stage, add Asiago and peas. Stir again and remove from heat.

3. **Cook pancetta** - While risotto is cooking, sauté pancetta in 1 teaspoon of olive oil until crispy. Alternatively, pancetta can be grilled while burgers are cooking.

4. **Heat grill to 400°.**

5. **Grill burgers about 3 to 4 minutes per side, or until cooked to preferred doneness.**

6. **While burgers are resting, warm cherry relish over medium heat. Add celery and cook 2 more minutes. Meanwhile, reheat risotto, adding a splash of stock and salt to taste. Stir in parsley moments before serving.**

7. **Serve, topping burgers with lettuce, pancetta and cherry relish.**

VENETO

TRADITIONAL PAIRINGS

	Noteworthy DOC(G)s and IGTs:	*Grape(s):*
Sparkling:	Prosecco di Conegliano-Valdobbiadene	Prosecco
White:	Soave, Soave Classico	Garganega
	Lugana	Trebbiano
	Bianco di Custoza	Garganega, Trebbiano
Red:	Valpolicella (including Ripasso and Amarone), Bardolino	Corvina, Rondinella, Molinara
	Veneto IGT	Corvina, Rondinella, Molinara, Cabernet Sauvignon and Cabernet Franc

---

ALTERNATE PAIRINGS

Whites and reds from neighboring Friuli-Venezia Giulia, Trentino-Alto Adige and Lombardy

Reds and whites from Austria

Reds from the Loire Valley in France

APPROPRIATE DESSERT WINE

Recioto Della Valpolicella

Recioto di Soave

EMILIA-ROMAGNA

How can a region that creates some of Italy's most culinarily advanced, refined and profound foodstuffs make such lousy wine? Put another way, could the land of Prosciutto di Parma, Aceto Balsamico Tradizionale di Modena (*authentic*, barrel-aged balsamic vinegar) and Parmigiano-Reggiano really be inhabited by people also willing to swill cheap Lambrusco with their artisanally crafted wares? In a word, no. The story is not so simple. From afar it would seem like Emilia-Romagna is a viticultural backwater, but the truth is closer to a reality shared by the (in)famous DOC of Soave in the nearby Veneto. For a long time, a handful of industrial brands were the only wines widely available for the U.S. market, offering a rather one-sided representation of what Emilia-Romagna is all about. Today, with a little effort, a greater variety of wines are within reach.

Glance at the map, and the purported state of things in Emilia-Romagna becomes even more unlikely. Bordered by Tuscany to the south and separated from the Veneto to the north by the Po River, this region is surrounded by producers of some of the country's greatest wines. In Bologna, Emilia-Romagna has an outstanding center for its food culture, a metropolis that is both center of gravity and defining point for the culture of the surrounding land, similar in role and stature to Genoa, Verona, Naples, even Rome. In terms of gastronomy, Emilia-Romagna is to Italy as Burgundy is to France. It is the belly of Italy, a land that may rank first in importance among twenty fiercely local- and quality-obsessed regions of this great peninsula.

To an outsider, the raw materials of Emilia-Romagna, many of which deserve the sort of diligent protection one would grant a UNESCO world heritage cultural site, make it a primary destination for any hungry tourist planning an Italian holiday. Nutty and creamy Prosciutto, made in the city of Parma, is to many the pinnacle of pork preparation, while artisanally made Parmigiano-Reggiano stands atop the list of the world's best cheeses. Balsamic vinegar from Modena offers an amusing paradox: although Emilia-Romagna is widely regarded as incapable of yielding wines of any great distinction, here, the pedestrian Trebbiano grape can be crafted into an elixir which can be more expensive on a per-milliliter basis than many of the world's greatest, most sought-after wines.

So, amid the praise for these extraordinary ingredients, the good wines got overlooked. A handful of diligent farmers maintained the regional wine traditions, away from the spotlight. As the name implies, this region is not uniform, actually broken into at least four distinct and important wine-growing areas, two of which are appended to form its moniker. Grapes like the white Albana and ubiquitous red Sangiovese make for compelling drinking, and in Emilia, Lambrusco reaches a greatness currently understood only by locals and a small band of international wine intelligentsia (known to outsiders as wine nerds). At the same time, many of Romagna's leading estates are pushing ahead with an increasing amount of quality French varietal bottlings; a familiar pattern that exists across much of the twenty-first century wine landscape. But back to Lambrusco: this misunderstood family of grapes can be made into white, *rosato* (rosé) or red wines. While sweet and fizzy versions are abundant, many compelling dry versions exist, often made lightly effervescent through secondary bottle fermentations, similar to *méthode ancestrale* wines from all over France. Today, to order this type of Lambrusco in a trendy wine bar is a way to show that you are a foodie/wine geek who is willing to seek authentic flavor at or beyond the boundaries of conventionally accepted "quality" wine zones.

MAJOR WHITE GRAPES:

Albana

Trebbiano

Malvasia

MAJOR RED GRAPES:

Lambrusco

Sangiovese

NOTEWORTHY SUB-REGIONS:

Albana di Romagna

Lambrusco Grasparossa di Castelvetro

Sangiovese di Romagna

EMILIA-ROMAGNA

Okay, so admittedly Emilia-Romagna is not the most highly regarded wine region. However, there must be an Emilia-Romagna burger, as it's the birthplace of a trifecta of the world's greatest ingredients: Prosciutto di Parma, Parmigiano-Reggiano and authentic balsamic vinegar. As the locals know, unheralded Lambrusco is an ideal choice to cut through the richness of Emilia-Romagna's decadent cuisine. It's also proof positive that inexpensive, uncomplicated wines can be a great addition to an immensely pleasurable feast!

RECOMMENDED COOKING METHOD: *Grill*   YIELDS: *4 servings*

BURGER INGREDIENTS:

1 ½ lbs ground beef

2 tbsp balsamic vinegar

2 tsp fresh thyme leaves

1 tsp salt

A note: Authentic, barrel-aged balsamic vinegar is significantly thicker than normal vinegar, almost syrupy, with a noticeable sweetness. It is essential to this recipe that you use the real thing, or one of the high quality vinegars made in the same style as opposed to thin, tart red wine vinegar with caramel coloring.

SPINACH RICOTTA:

⅓ cup ricotta

2 cups spinach, chopped

1 tbsp butter

ASSEMBLE WITH:

4 burger buns, split

8 slices prosciutto, sautéed

Shaved Parmigiano-Reggiano

Spinach ricotta

SIDE DISH BALSAMIC ROASTED CARROTS:

1 ½ lbs carrots, peeled and trimmed

2 tbsp balsamic vinegar

1 tbsp olive oil

1 tsp salt

TO PREPARE

1. **Prep carrots** - Toss carrots with balsamic vinegar, olive oil and salt and place on a baking sheet.

2. **Prep spinach ricotta** - In a large sauté pan over medium heat, sauté spinach in butter for about 90 seconds, or until it has wilted and released its liquid. Remove from heat, drain off all but 1 teaspoon of the liquid and add ricotta. Stir and set aside.

3. **Combine burger ingredients** - Gently mix beef, balsamic vinegar, thyme and salt. Form burgers and set aside.

4. Gather buns and toppings, set aside.

Use a cheese slicer or vegetable peeler to shave the Parmigiano-Reggiano to the perfect thickness.

COOK & SERVE

1. Preheat oven to 350°. Roast carrots 25 - 30 minutes, or until tender and caramelized.

2. Grill or sauté prosciutto in olive oil until crispy.

3. Heat grill to 400°.

4. Grill burgers 3 to 4 minutes per side, or until cooked to preferred doneness. Beef will be well caramelized due to the balsamic vinegar.

5. Serve, topping burgers with shaved Parmigiano-Reggiano, prosciutto and spinach ricotta.

TRADITIONAL PAIRINGS

	Noteworthy DOC(G)s:	*Grape(s):*
Red:	Lambrusco di Sorbara,	Lambrusco
	Lambrusco Grasparossa di Castelvetro,	
	Lambrusco Salamino di Santa Croce	
	Sangiovese di Romagna	Sangiovese
	Colli Bolognesi	Cabernet Sauvignon, Barbera
	Colli Piacentini	Bonarda, Barbera, Pinot Nero

ALTERNATE PAIRINGS

Red wines from neighboring Le Marche, Tuscany and Veneto

Sparkling Shiraz from Australia

Bonarda from Argentina

APPROPRIATE DESSERT WINE

Vin Santo from neighboring Tuscany

TUSCANY

Tuscany spreads across 9,000 square miles, bordered on the west by the Mediterranean Sea and to the east by the Appenine mountain range, which runs Italy's length and is often referred to as its backbone. Its land is hilly, covered by an agricultural patchwork of grapes, olives, grains and more, with Chianti and a vast number of Sangiovese vines lying at the heart of it all.

Italy's most famous wine's reputation has swung the full arc from standard-bearer to goat and back several times since its zone was established in the fourteenth century. The original core of Chianti is the Classico zone, which is surrounded by modern subzones sprawling across central Tuscany, including Montalbano, Colli Senesi and Colli Fiorentini. The creation and expansion of these Chianti suburbs originated from economic pressure having little to do with quality, and much to do with the ease of selling a bottle labeled as Chianti. Wines from these satellite Chianti zones can be very good, but it would be a stretch to say they share the terroir of the original nucleus. The old-timers had a reason for their demarcation.

South of the Chianti zones lies the village of Montalcino, which has experienced a century-long growth in relevance, now yielding one of Italy's most important wines. Brunello di Montalcino has been legendary since its creation by Clemente Santi and his grandson Ferruccio Biondi-Santi. It is a single-varietal wine made from the local Sangiovese Grosso grape (referred to there as Brunello, which translates to "nice dark one") and aged for several years in oak barrels prior to release. It got its start as a secret wine, made exclusively by Biondi-Santi and released only in stellar vintages. Prior to 1950, the Biondi Santi estate sold bottles exclusively from 1888, 1891, 1924 and 1945. Now things have changed. Montalcino's wines are still among Italy's most expensive, despite widespread availability (150 estates make 3.6 million bottles annually), thanks in part to high critical praise.

A hillside away to the east sits the town of Montepulciano (not to be confused with the grape of the same name that is grown in Abruzzo), an example of what Montalcino may have been if its residents had rested on their laurels. Historically listed as one of the "big three" red wine zones of Tuscany, along with the above two DOCGs, few wine scribes seem able to mention Montepulciano without the word "underachiever" somewhere nearby. The name of its great wine, Vino Nobile di Montepulciano, betrays pretentions and potential that's rarely delivered. Despite negative aspects, it bears noting that quality is on the rise, with some of the region's best estates moving toward higher percentages of a local Sangiovese clone known as Prugnolo Gentile.

Throughout Tuscany, several international grapes have risen the ranks to stardom, particularly Cabernet Sauvignon, Merlot and Syrah. The most notable area is Bolgheri, located on the Tuscan coastline, where these foreign grapes are usually blended with Sangiovese to make many popular Super-Tuscans. The Maremma, home to Bolgheri (as well as the Sangiovese-based Morellino di Scansano DOCG), is quite warm, which allows the grapes greater ripeness than those grown in more inland Tuscan vineyards. The finished wines from this prestigious outpost have a bigness and polish that has garnered a strong following among serious wine collectors.

White wine is frequently an afterthought when pontificating about the greatness of Tuscan wines, but it's an essential precursor to the ultimate Fiorentino feast. Trebbiano and Vermentino make up the bulk of white plantings in Tuscany, while Vernaccia is responsible for the region's sole white DOCG wine, in the town of San Gimignano. Tuscan whites are *aperitivos* through and through; clean and crisp, great for casual quaffing with antipasti, but rarely offering any great moments of vinous enlightenment. When dinnertime kicks into high gear out come the reds. Vin Santo, Tuscany's dessert wine made from Trebbiano and Malvasia, is a perfect conclusion to the meal when served with a plate of almond biscotti.

MAJOR WHITE GRAPES:

Trebbiano

Vermentino

Vernaccia

Malvasia

MAJOR RED GRAPES:

Sangiovese

Cabernet Sauvignon

Merlot

NOTEWORTHY SUB-REGIONS:

Brunello di Montalcino

Chianti

Chianti Classico

Bolgheri

Vino Nobile di Montepulciano

Morellino di Scansano

Vernaccia di San Gimignano

The Tuscany Burger was a fun one to create because it merges America's most iconic food with the cuisine that is identified as being so quintessentially Italian. Sun-dried tomatoes, olives, pancetta and Pecorino cheese all come together in this easy, delicious recipe. Sage-roasted cauliflower adds some rustic charm to this meal, which is great with anything from a simple Sangiovese Toscana all the way up to a well-aged Brunello di Montalcino.

RECOMMENDED COOKING METHOD: *Grill*   YIELDS: *4 servings*

BURGER INGREDIENTS:

1 ¼ lbs ground beef

¼ cup Tuscan tapenade (see below)

½ cup grated Pecorino Toscano
(or Pecorino Romano)

2 tbsp finely chopped sage

TUSCAN TAPENADE:

⅔ cup whole, pitted green olives

⅔ cup oil-packed sun-dried tomatoes

1 tbsp extra virgin olive oil, or as needed

1 clove garlic

ASSEMBLE WITH:

4 burger buns, split

4 - 8 slices pancetta (or bacon)

4 tomato slices

Arugula

Tuscan tapenade

SIDE DISH SAGE ROASTED CAULIFLOWER:

Florets from 1 head of cauliflower

2 tbsp olive oil

1 tsp salt

2 tbsp finely chopped sage

¼ cup grated Pecorino Toscano
(or Pecorino Romano)

Pinch of red pepper flakes

TO PREPARE

1. **Make Tuscan tapenade** - Combine green olives, sun-dried tomatoes, olive oil and garlic in a food processor and blend to a smooth paste. Add more olive oil if necessary, about 1 teaspoon at a time, to achieve a smooth texture. Set aside.

2. **Prep cauliflower** - In a large mixing bowl, toss cauliflower in olive oil, salt, sage, parsley and red pepper flakes until all florets are seasoned. Spread cauliflower out on a baking sheet, and sprinkle with the Pecorino.

3. **Combine burger ingredients** - Combine beef, Pecorino, parsley, sage and ¼ cup of the tapenade and mix gently. Form burgers and set aside.

4. **Gather buns and toppings, set aside.**

COOK & SERVE

1. **Roast cauliflower** - Preheat oven to 375°. Roast cauliflower in oven for about 40 minutes, or until florets are soft and the Pecorino is golden brown.

2. **Heat grill to 400°.**

3. **Cook pancetta** - Grill or sauté 1 to 3 slices of pancetta per burger, depending on how thick or thin the pancetta is sliced. Cook until slightly crispy.

4. **Grill burgers 3 to 4 minutes per side, or until cooked to preferred doneness.**

5. **Serve, topping burgers with pancetta, tomato, arugula and tapenade.**

TUSCANY

TRADITIONAL PAIRINGS

	Noteworthy DOC(G)s and IGTs:	*Grape(s):*
Red:	Brunello di Montalcino	Brunello (Sangiovese Grosso)
	Chianti, Chianti Classico	Sangiovese, Canaiolo, Up to 15% non-indigenous grapes
	Bolgheri	Cabernet Sauvignon, Merlot, Sangiovese, Cabernet Franc, Syrah
	Vino Nobile di Montepulciano	Prugnolo Gentile (Sangiovese), Canaiolo, up to 20% non-indigenous grapes
	Morellino di Scansano	Morellino (Sangiovese)
	Montecucco	Sangiovese
	Tuscany IGT	Sangiovese, Cabernet Sauvignon, Merlot, Syrah

Various reds labeled as Rosso (Toscano Rosso, Rosso di Montalcino, etc), based largely on Sangiovese.

ALTERNATE PAIRINGS

Reds from nearby Umbria, Le Marche, Abruzzo and Molise

Sangiovese from California and Australia

Red wines from Bordeaux, France

APPROPRIATE DESSERT WINE

Vin Santo, made from partially dried Trebbiano and Malvasia

CAMPANIA

For decades, Campania has been a mere footnote to a thorough study of Italian wine. The entire region, including its wine culture, has been dragged down by poverty, pollution and crime, overshadowing the great culinary traditions of this agriculturally privileged land. Despite Naples' amazing pizza, panini and architecture, it's a city most travelers are just passing through on their way to the awe-inspiring panoramas of Campania's Amalfi Coast. This unspoiled area is a tourist mecca, complete with lemon groves, azure water and seafood: a snapshot of the good life.

Despite every hindrance, Campania is unquestionably home to the finest cheeses and wines made south of Rome. Creamy, silky Burrata brings fresh cheese to a new level of decadence, while Aglianico takes red wine to dark places few other varietals are capable of exploring. This ancient Greek grape variety yields some of Italy's finest reds outside of Piedmont and Tuscany, yet manages to fly far under the radar of most wine drinkers. Southern Italy's most important white grape, Greco, also thrives in Campania since arriving with the Greeks nearly three thousand years ago.

So why is a region with a millennial history of grape cultivation not among Italy's more important wine-producing regions? Simply put, much of Campania's land is too fertile to make interesting wines. Crops as varied as strawberries, tomatoes and chestnuts find the rich soils, warm summers and plentiful rainfall ideal for turning out abundant yields of tasty produce, but vines produce better quality fruit when they are forced to struggle for their sustenance. However, a revolution against mediocrity in Campania's wine industry began in the early 1990s, and amazing potential is being realized once again. Aglianico grapes, grown in the cool volcanic soils of high-elevation sites, are often the latest-picked red grapes in Europe for dry wine production. Long growing cycles allow for exceptional aromatic complexity and age-worthiness in Taurasi and other Aglianico-based wines. The simplest of these wines are dominated by aromas of fresh berries, plums and spice, and are deliciously juicy when young. More serious examples are brooding, brawny and tannic, packed with tar, licorice and black cherry flavors and are unmistakably reminiscent of the dark, minerally soil in which the grapes are grown. These require significant time in the cellar. Blends that feature a high percentage of the indigenous Piedirosso grape make for more immediately enjoyable drinking, thanks to its soft tannins and fresh acidity.

In recent years, Campania has also become a shining star for Italian white wines, a category largely overlooked by most wine drinkers, not counting the ocean of forgettable Pinot Grigio consumed annually in America. Greco, Falanghina and Fiano form the trio of interesting whites which pair beautifully with the bounty of seafood pulled from the Tyrrhenian Sea, particularly with lightly grilled calamari or steamed clams with garlic and a knob of parsley butter. When properly handled, these wines are bright, pure and fresh, with citrusy flavors reminiscent of Sauvignon Blanc and Albariño. But because these grapes are especially susceptible to oxidation, a richer and fuller-bodied representation of these wines exists, with a waxy quality and golden color. Regardless of style, most of these whites have crisp acid, pleasant minerality, show floral aromas and are largely unoaked. Most bottlings are at their best as close to release as possible, usually within a year or two of the vintage date.

All the components for great wine with a distinct southern character are here, and ambitious winemakers from northern Italy and beyond are beginning to take notice. Investment, modernization and exploration of the rich legacy of genetic materials that have existed here for centuries are beginning again.

MAJOR WHITE GRAPES:

Falanghina

Fiano

Greco

MAJOR RED GRAPES:

Aglianico

NOTEWORTHY SUB-REGIONS:

Taurasi

Fiano di Avellino

Greco di Tufo

Taburno

Home to Caprese salad and Neapolitan pizza, Campania has more to offer than just basil, mozzarella and tomato. This tasty combo of pork, capers, basil, provolone and roasted red peppers is easy to whip together, and goes great with Campania's delicious white wines and one of Italy's most underrated reds, Aglianico. Campania's famous combination of ingredients also deserves to be represented here, so I suggest serving the Campania burger with a traditional Caprese salad, using only the finest tomatoes when they're in season.

RECOMMENDED COOKING METHOD: *Grill*   YIELDS: *4 servings*

BURGER INGREDIENTS:

1 ¼ lbs ground pork

¼ cup finely chopped basil

2 tbsp lightly chopped capers

2 tbsp tomato paste

2 cloves minced garlic

½ tsp red pepper flakes

1 tsp salt

ASSEMBLE WITH:

4 burger buns, split

Provolone cheese slices

Roasted red bell pepper (2 peppers, if roasting your own)

Basil leaves (approximately 5 large leaves per burger)

SIDE DISH CAPRESE SALAD:

2 medium tomatoes

1 large ball of fresh mozzarella

1 cup basil, lightly chopped

Olive oil, salt and pepper to taste

TO PREPARE

1. **Combine burger ingredients** - Gently mix pork, basil, capers, tomato paste, garlic, red pepper flakes and salt in a large mixing bowl. Form burgers and set aside.

2. **Roast peppers (if roasting your own)** - Preheat grill or oven to 450°. Roast the peppers, turning as needed until the skin is charred on all sides, about 10 minutes in total. When done, immediately place the peppers in a paper bag or a bowl covered with plastic wrap for 15 minutes. Peel off the skin and remove the stem and seeds. Cut into medium-sized strips and set aside.

3. **Assemble Caprese salad** - On a large serving tray, alternately layer slices of tomato and mozzarella. Top with basil. Just before serving, drizzle with olive oil and sprinkle with salt and pepper to taste.

4. **Gather buns and toppings, set aside.**

COOK & SERVE

1. **Heat grill to 400°.**

2. **Grill burgers 3 to 4 minutes per side, or until cooked to preferred doneness. Add Provolone during final minute of cooking.**

3. **Serve, topping burgers with basil and roasted red bell peppers.**

CAMPANIA

TRADITIONAL PAIRINGS

	Noteworthy DOC(G)s and IGTs:	*Grape(s):*
White:	Fiano di Avellino	Fiano
	Greco di Tufo	Greco
	Blends and varietally-labeled whites made from Fiano, Falanghina, Greco, Pallagrello Bianco and Biancolella	
Red:	Taurasi	Aglianico
	Aglianico del Taburno	Aglianico
	Red blends and varietally-labeled wines made from Aglianico, Piedirosso and Cabernet Sauvignon	

ALTERNATE PAIRINGS

Whites and reds from neighboring Lazio, Puglia, Basilica and Calabria

Greek whites and reds

Arneis from Piedmont, Italy

APPROPRIATE DESSERT WINE

Marsala from nearby Sicily

SICILY

For decades, Sicily was Italy's most productive wine region. In most vintages as much as fifty percent of the harvest was used in the production of Marsala, particularly the Grillo and Catarratto grapes that are grown on the western extreme of the island, near Trapani. Another significant portion would end up as "cutting wine," adding pigmentation and body to anemic reds from colder regions of the Italian mainland and France. This fraudulent practice continues into the twenty-first century, but most likely reached its height in the 1960s and '70s. In contrast to the rich culinary history of the island, most Sicilian wine was either bland white from Alcamo or unfocused, rustic red from Mt. Etna and elsewhere.

This quality dichotomy has more to do with the failures of post-World War II agrarian reform than any intention on the part of Sicilian farmers to make shoddy wine. In 1946, the new Italian republic seized large tracts of land from the oppressive patriarchs of the *latifondo* system and gave it to farmers whose families had been landless peasants. However, the parcels were generally too small to justify building a cellar, so cooperative winemaking facilities sprouted across the island to help farmers vinify grapes and bottle their wine. The main problem with large-scale co-op winemaking is that it tends to emphasize quantity over quality, paying members by the ton with little emphasis on ripeness. Growers plant the most vigorous varieties, making technically correct, but soulless, one-dimensional wines with an absence of local character. The anonymity of these wines led to the beginning of what is likely to be a long, slow death for the co-op system across southern Europe. These facilities are poorly positioned to compete with corporate New World wineries also prepared to churn out inexpensive product, often with better marketing and a fruitier, more accessible flavor profile.

In today's Sicily, cultivated acreage and total wine production drops annually. This is a good thing. Between 1992 and 2002, total production on the island fell by 40 percent, shedding much of the co-op plonk. In the early years of the twenty-first century it appears possible that Sicily will reposition itself in the marketplace as a home for ambitious, quality wine estates. For one thing, it's one of the few areas of Italy with affordable land if you're interested in starting a wine endeavor. Sadly, too many of these new domains

SICILY

opt to use lots of new oak and über-sexy packaging to separate themselves from the bad old days of the co-ops. Instead of showcasing Sicilian terroir, they make facsimiles of $30-$50 Napa or Aussie wines for roughly the same price. However, a promising new Sicily is emerging. The indigenous white grape Inzolia is made into a soft, refreshing, inviting wine that provides Chardonnay drinkers a pleasing change of pace, while the bright strawberry and raspberry flavors found in Nero d'Avola and Frappato offer a better glimpse into the *real* Sicily than any of the "international varieties" grown on the island.

It may seem that the sun-baked region is well suited to wines of California-style bigness, but Sicily's variety of terrain and climate are surprising. Just drive around Etna and you'll see high-elevation arable land and vines as verdant as in northern France. The Baroque hilltop towns of Sicily's southeastern corner provide the elevation and proximity to cooling sea breezes necessary for wines with both ripeness and acid structure. In short, the Sicily=Hot equation is too simplified to be useful. Some new estates are seeking fragrance, balance and traditional flavor in their wines, showcasing a side of Sicily that's likely to win admirers in the years ahead.

MAJOR WHITE GRAPES:

Catarratto

Inzolia

Grecanico

Grillo

Malvasia

MAJOR RED GRAPES:

Nero d'Avola

Frappato

Cabernet Sauvignon

Syrah

NOTEWORTHY SUB-REGIONS:

Marsala

Cerasuolo di Vittoria

Etna

SICILY

Sicilian cuisine is far more varied than one might expect of a small island. Outside influences are evident in Sicilian cooking, which incorporates Arab, North African and Greek ingredients in many of its dishes. For the Sicily Burger, the focus is on the seafood of the coast and the citrus fruits for which the island is so renowned. Sweet and savory components come together in both the burger and the side dish to complement the island's fresh and juicy wines.

RECOMMENDED COOKING METHOD: **Non-stick sauté pan**   YIELDS: **4 servings**

BURGER INGREDIENTS:

1 ¼ lbs finely chopped fresh tuna, skin removed

6 oz jar oil-packed artichoke hearts, drained

3 tbsp capers

¼ cup finely diced fennel stalk

1 tsp salt

CITRUS RICOTTA:

½ cup orange juice

½ cup ricotta

¼ tsp salt

ASSEMBLE WITH:

4 burger buns, split

1 fennel bulb, thinly sliced

Citrus Ricotta

SIDE DISH CHILLED COUSCOUS WITH CITRUS VINAIGRETTE:

½ cup plain couscous

1 ¼ cup vegetable broth or water

1 tbsp butter

Segments of 1 orange, cut into bite-sized chunks

¼ cup sliced almonds, toasted

¼ cup sliced black olives

¼ cup parsley, lightly chopped

Salt to taste

CITRUS VINAGRETTE:

2 tbsp olive oil

1 tbsp white wine vinegar

2 tbsp orange juice

Juice of 1 small lemon (about 2 tbsp)

1 tsp honey

Salt and pepper to taste

TO PREPARE

1. **Make couscous and citrus vinaigrette** - Bring broth or water to a boil with 1 tablespoon of butter. Add couscous and turn heat off. Cover and let sit 5 minutes. Fluff couscous and transfer to a large mixing bowl. Meanwhile, in a dry sauté pan, toast almonds until lightly browned. Add to couscous with orange segments, black olives and parsley. Salt to taste. Refrigerate until burgers are ready to serve.

In a small bowl, whisk together olive oil, white wine vinegar, orange juice, lemon juice and honey. Add salt and pepper to taste. Set aside.

2. **Combine burger ingredients** - Cut tuna into 1-inch chunks, and chop in a small food processor along with artichoke hearts until no large chunks remain. Try to avoid grinding tuna to a paste. Transfer to a mixing bowl and combine with capers, fennel and salt. Form into burgers and refrigerate until you are ready to cook.

3. **Gather buns and toppings, set aside.**

COOK & SERVE

1. **Make citrus ricotta** - In a small saucepan, reduce orange juice to a syrup (about 1 tablespoon). Remove from heat and mix in ricotta and salt.

2. **Cook burgers** - Place a large sauté pan on medium-high heat. Add 1 to 2 tablespoons olive oil, and gently place burgers in pan. Cook to preferred doneness, being careful not to overcook tuna.

3. **Serve, topping burgers with shaved fennel and citrus ricotta.**

4. **Serve couscous salad, dressed with citrus vinaigrette.**

SICILY

TRADITIONAL PAIRINGS

In Sicily, DOC wines are of relatively little importance compared to those of the rest of Italy. Varietally-labeled wines and proprietary blends are far more common on the shelves of most reputable retailers in the U.S. Look for wines made from the following grapes:

White: Inzolia (Insolia)

Grecanico

Chardonnay

Grillo

Catarratto

Red: Frappato

Nero d'Avola

ALTERNATE PAIRINGS

Vermentino from nearby Sardinia

Whites from Greece

Albariño from Galicia, Spain

APPROPRIATE DESSERT WINE

Marsala

SPAIN

If the idea of learning French and Italian wine makes you feel like you're jumping into the deep end of the pool, then perhaps Spain offers an easier entry point on your quest to learn about Europe's best wines. Spanish wines are a little more accepting of the broad generalizations that simply won't fly in France and Italy. There are far fewer prominent grapes grown in Spain, with Garnacha and Tempranillo taking up large market share among reds, followed by Monastrell, Bobal and Cariñena. A handful of important white grape varieties are conveniently lumped together in the crisp-and-refreshing category, led by Albariño and Macabeo (also known as Viura). Airén, the world's most planted grape, is largely used for distillation, while Palomino is used primarily for producing Sherry. Additionally, there are a slew of well-crafted, sub-$20 bottles coming out of virtually every corner of Spain, so it's one of the more wallet-friendly learning experiences.

As you've surely learned by now, when speaking of wine, exceptions always exist. The same factors that make Spanish wines so accessible can simultaneously handicap the learning process. Because so many winegrowing regions focus on a narrow group of grape varieties, there exists a homogeneity that can make it hard to decipher the unique identity of a region. The list currently exceeds sixty winegrowing regions and seems to grow daily.

Like France's AOC and Italy's DOC, Spain has the Denominación de Origen (DO), and the top tier Denominación de Origen Calificada (DOCa, or DOQ in Catalan), which govern the boundaries of each region, the grapes that may be used in a wine bearing that DO's name and certain aging criteria. The DO-regulated terms Crianza, Reserva and Gran Reserva indicate successively longer barrel and bottle aging minimums prior to release. Conversely, a wine labeled Joven has spent little or no time in barrel before release.

Vino de la Tierra and Vino de Mesa, Spain's equivalent to France's Vin de Pays and Italy's IGT, cover those areas that are not currently classified as DOs, and allow for production of wines containing non-sanctioned grapes. While many wines are labeled according to their place-name, or DO, it is not uncommon to see the grape variety or blend on a bottle's front or back label.

GALICIA

Galicia is a verdant area, scenic in a way that is at times reminiscent of Ireland or Norway. Rivers cut deeply into the rolling landscape, while the coast is jagged, wet and cold. Its people have a history of hauling a livelihood from the water, but away from the coast this is the least prosperous region in the country. Many emigrated away to more economically promising parts of Spain and abroad throughout the nineteenth century. Above Portugal, perched on the edge of the Atlantic Ocean, Galicia does not fit the visual stereotype of Spain. Inland, and disconnected from well known white-wine-producing areas on the west Galician coast, vineyards are so steep that dumbwaiters are often used to lower fruit down from the vines. Despite this daunting physical obstacle, grapevines have been cultivated across Galicia since Roman times.

Galicia is separated from the rest of Spain by the Sierra de Ancares mountain range, and subsequently has grown and developed its culture in relative isolation. Known as "The Green Spain," this northern land is cooler and wetter than any other part of Iberia. It is closer to Portugal geographically and culturally than to Madrid. The people of Galicia speak a language called Gallego, a hybrid of Castilian Spanish and Portuguese. In the streets of Galicia's capital you'll hear the skirl of bagpipes, a result of the area's early Celtic inhabitants and a reminder that we are culturally about as far away from flamenco music and the sunny, dry landscapes of southern Spain as you could possibly be.

So, why is Galicia important to us? For starters, the wines made in this remote corner of Spain are so stylistically different than those from the rest of the country. The unique landscape and climate have done good things for the Albariño grape, a star in the region, particularly in Rías Baixas, Galicia's most important D.O. It has been so successful, in fact, that Rías Baixas is arguably the top source of white wine in the entire country, even attaining a degree of cult status. Wines made from the Albariño grape are at once clean, crisp and lemony as well as full, ripe and tropical. Not surprisingly, these wines are the ideal match for the dizzying array of seafood that is regularly found on a Gallegan dinner table, including tuna, octopus, mussels, razor clams, oysters, scallops and crabs. Seafood is omnipresent here, and of such exceptional quality that a canning industry grew around it in the mid-1800s. The industry has been so successful that Galician-owned canning operations have sprouted up across the globe.

White grapes Treixadura, Torrontés, Loureira and Albillo are also well suited to the cool, damp climate of Galicia, though none have reached the heights of Albariño. It's hard to classify a region with over 2,500 years of winemaking history as an up-and-comer; nevertheless, whites from the Ribeiro and Valdeorras DOs are on the rise and may give those from Rías Baixas a run for their money in the coming years.

It's fitting that the region which produces Spain's standout white wine would also yield a red wine unlike most of the country's more popular *tintos*. Reds from Galicia remain a treasure yet to be discovered by most, but that is sure to change soon. The Mencía grape is making a name for itself in Ribeira Sacra, as well as on the other side of the Ancares Mountains in Bierzo, just outside of Galicia, in Castile. Generally speaking it has high acid, which gives its wines an alluring elegance, even in those made in a dense, extracted style. It offers a wonderful pairing for the cuisine that originates away from Galicia's coast.

MAJOR WHITE GRAPES:

Albariño

Godello

Loureira

MAJOR RED GRAPES:

Mencía

NOTEWORTHY SUB-REGIONS:

Rías Baixas

Ribeira Sacra

Ribeiro

Valdeorras

GALICIA

Sometimes the most obvious selection of starting ingredients doesn't result in the best burger. Such was the case in the creation of the Galicia Burger. Gallegan cuisine is dominated by seafood, which – depending on the ingredient – doesn't always translate well into burger form, so instead you get a little surf-and-turf with a chicken burger and a fried seafood salad on the side. Albariño is the natural choice to pair with the meal, but don't overlook Galicia's up-and-coming red wines.

RECOMMENDED COOKING METHOD: *Cast iron pan*   **YIELDS:** *4 servings*

BURGER INGREDIENTS:

1 ¼ lbs ground chicken, preferably dark meat

½ cup finely chopped onion

2 tbsp finely chopped parsley

½ tsp sweet paprika

½ tsp ground cumin

1 tsp salt

Breadcrumbs as needed

SOFRITO:

½ cup finely chopped onion

1 15-oz can diced tomatoes, drained

1 clove minced garlic

1 tbsp olive oil

½ tsp sweet paprika

¼ tsp salt

WILTED TURNIP GREENS:

6 cups chopped turnip greens (or other hearty green), ribs removed

1 tbsp butter

¼ tsp salt

Water, as needed

ASSEMBLE WITH:

4 burger buns, split

Tetilla cheese or Brie

Wilted turnip greens

Sofrito

SIDE DISH FRIED SEAFOOD SALAD:

3 oz can mussels

1 egg

2 tbsp milk

½ cup flour

½ medium onion, thinly sliced

1 small serrano pepper, thinly sliced and seeds removed

1 large tomato, cut into 8 slices

4 oz green beans, cut into 1-inch pieces

Juice of 1 lemon

3 tbsp olive oil, more for sautéing

Sea salt

TO PREPARE

1. **Prep turnip greens** - Pull leaves off of ribs, chop and rinse. Discard ribs.

2. **Combine burger ingredients** - Gently mix chicken, onion, parsley, paprika, cumin and salt in a large mixing bowl. Add breadcrumbs as needed until you can easily form the burgers without the chicken sticking to your hands. Form burgers and set aside.

3. **Prep seafood salad ingredients** - Whisk egg and milk together in a bowl, add mussels and stir to coat. Remove mussels and dredge in flour. Toss mussels in a sieve to remove excess flour.

Bring a small saucepan of water to a boil. Add green beans and blanch for about 1 minute. Drain and submerge in an ice bath to stop the cooking. Set aside.

4. **Gather buns and toppings, set aside.**

COOK & SERVE

1. **Make sofrito** - In a medium saucepan, sweat onions in olive oil over low heat until they begin to soften. Add garlic and paprika, and cook another 2 minutes before adding drained tomatoes and salt. Simmer 15-20 minutes, stirring occasionally.

2. **Wilt turnip greens** - Place a large saucepan on medium-high heat. Add butter, chopped turnip greens and salt. Stir, adding water as needed until greens have softened considerably, approximately 10 minutes.

3. **Cook mussels; assemble salad**- Set a medium sauté pan over medium-high heat, with enough olive oil to coat the bottom of the pan. Add mussels and serrano pepper. Sauté until mussels are brown and crispy.

Assemble salad with tomato, onion and green beans, topped with mussels and peppers. Drizzle with lemon juice and olive oil. Sprinkle with a high quality sea salt.

4. **Preheat a large cast iron pan or skillet on a 375° grill or on a stovetop burner set to medium-high heat. Drizzle the pan with vegetable oil just before adding burgers.**

5. **Cook burgers 3 to 4 minutes per side, or until cooked to preferred doneness.**

6. **Serve, topping burgers with wilted turnip greens, sofrito and Tetilla or Brie.**

GALICIA

TRADITIONAL PAIRINGS

	Noteworthy DOs:	*Grape(s):*
White:	Rías Baixas	Albariño, Loureira, Godello, Treixadura
	Ribeira Sacra	Albariño, Godello
	Ribeiro	Treixadura
	Valdeorras	Godello
Red:	Ribeira Sacra	Mencía

ALTERNATE PAIRINGS

White and rosé Txakoli from the nearby Basque country

White wines from France's Gascogne region

Torrontés from Argentina

APPROPRIATE DESSERT WINE

Port, from neighboring Portugal

CASTILE AND LEÓN

Spain is far more culturally varied than our shorthand image of it. That said, the region of Castile and León is at the center of the dominant Spanish cultural identity. Via its capital, Madrid, Castilian food and wine culture spread throughout Iberia and the world. Along with Rioja, the great reds of this area are the modern archetypes of Spanish wine. One expects their flavors when ordering a glass of Spanish red in a restaurant, far more so than the varied profiles of so many of Spain's other winemaking regions.

Castile and León is a large area, stretching from Galicia and Portugal on the west all the way to Rioja on the east. Arid conditions and ideal soils make the region a haven free of numerous vine maladies that afflict most other grape-growing areas. The reds from this region are made largely from the Tempranillo grape, a native that gets its euphonious name from a tendency to ripen *temprano*, early. Under a variety of names, the grape does good things across Spain, particularly in sites with decent drainage and significant diurnal temperature variation. In most instances, the ripe Tempranillo grape shows physical traits that are borne out in the flavors of the finished wine: thick-skinned and dark in color, it's easy to imagine. In Ribera Del Duero, it reaches heights seldom achieved in most other parts of the world.

Ribera del Duero, meaning "banks of the Duero" (as in Duero River), is certainly the most well known winegrowing sub-region of Castile and León, a large chunk of land located in north-central Spain. In the last quarter century, this region has caught the imagination of wine drinkers around the world, due in part to the legendary Vega Sicilia estate, which dates back to 1864, as well as to a host of new, high-quality wineries including Pesquera, Pingus and Sastre. Wine has been made here since at least the thirteenth century. Despite its high reputation, DO status was not awarded until 1982. It was elevated to the more prestigious DOCa status in 2008. There's good reason for this honor: high alpine valleys allow for a 120-plus day ripening season, which is great for developing complex flavors and longevity, hallmarks which have made the red wines of Ribera del Duero famous. Many vines are over seventy-five years of age, yielding dense, concentrated juice. Few regions in Spain are capable of creating wines of such stellar quality.

The Toro appellation was awarded DO status five years after Ribera Del Duero, and makes similarly styled, if slightly less-refined reds from the Tempranillo grape, known here as Tinto de Toro. The region is warmer than Ribera Del Duero, which explains their brawnier style. Numanthia is the standard-bearer for the region, along with the more recently established Pintia winery, owned by Vega Sicilia. Cigales, to the north, is the most recent noteworthy DO in the region, created in 1991. Here, Tempranillo goes by the name Tinta del País, and is joined by Garnacha to make reds and a handful of *rosados* (rosés).

Wines from Bierzo have little in common with those from the rest of Castile and León, not surprising given the distance between this remote outpost and its counterparts. Tempranillo takes a back seat to the Mencía grape in Bierzo, which is located at the western edge of Castile and León, separated from Galicia by the Sierra dos Ancares mountain range. Bierzo wines have more blueberry and blackberry fruit aromas, as well as more minerality than their Tempranillo-based cousins. They run the gamut from light and elegant to dark and sturdy. Look out for Bierzo as an emerging appellation of interest.

White wine production in Castile and León is concentrated in the DO of Rueda, where Verdejo and Viura are the grapes of choice. Any fan of Sauvignon Blanc needs to give one of these refreshing thirst-quenchers a try. Outside of Rueda, wines made from Albillo and Malvasía offer comparable drinking experiences, ideal for summer sipping on the deck while you fire up the grill to cook the Castile and León Burger!

MAJOR WHITE GRAPES:

Verdejo

Viura

Albillo

MAJOR RED GRAPES:

Tinto Fino
(Tempranillo)

Tinto de Toro
(Tempranillo)

Tinta del País
(Tempranillo)

Mencía

Garnacha

NOTEWORTHY SUB-REGIONS:

Ribera Del Duero

Toro

Bierzo

Cigales

Rueda

Simplicity at its finest, the Castile and León Burger is a spin on cordero asado, or roast lamb, a specialty of the Castilian kitchen. Just because it's easy to make doesn't mean it isn't good…and I mean crazy good. Suckling lamb is a favorite pairing with the local reds, and this burger will show you why. For even more flavor, cook the burgers in a searing-hot cast iron pan over a hardwood charcoal fire with some smoking chips, and baste the burgers every couple minutes with their own cumin-infused juices.

RECOMMENDED COOKING METHOD: *Cast iron pan over grill*   YIELDS: *4 servings*

BURGER INGREDIENTS:

1 ½ lbs ground lamb

1 tbsp ground cumin

1 tbsp finely chopped oregano

1 clove minced garlic

1 tsp salt

CHICKPEA SPREAD:

1 cup chickpeas, drained

3 tbsp olive oil for sautéing, more or as needed

1 tsp ground cumin

¼ tsp salt

ASSEMBLE WITH:

4 burger buns, split

Thinly sliced cabbage

Zamorano or Manchego cheese slices

Chickpea spread

SIDE DISH SAUTÉED CABBAGE AND CHICKPEAS:

3 cups shredded cabbage

1 15-oz can chickpeas, drained

2 tbsp olive oil

½ tsp paprika

½ tsp salt

TO PREPARE

1. **Make chickpea spread** - Sauté chickpeas and ground cumin in olive oil over medium heat until lightly browned. Combine chickpeas and olive oil with salt in a small food processor, and purée until smooth. Add more olive oil as needed to create a smooth texture.

2. **Combine burger ingredients** - In a large mixing bowl, gently combine the lamb, oregano, garlic, cumin and salt. Form burgers and set aside.

3. **Gather buns and toppings, set aside.**

COOK & SERVE

1. **Sauté cabbage and chickpeas** - Place a large sauté pan on medium-high heat with 2 tablespoons of olive oil. Add chickpeas, cabbage, paprika and salt. Cook about 5 minutes, stirring occasionally, until chickpeas have browned slightly and cabbage has softened. Reduce heat to lowest setting.

2. **Heat grill to 450˚.**

3. **Grill burgers 3 to 4 minutes per side, or until cooked to preferred doneness.**

4. **Serve, topping burgers with Zamorano or Manchego cheese, cabbage and chickpea spread.**

TRADITIONAL PAIRINGS

	Noteworthy DOs:	*Grape(s):*
Red:	Ribera Del Duero	Tinto Fino
	Toro	Tinta de Toro, Garnacha
	Cigales	Tinta de País, Garnacha Tinta
	Bierzo	Mencía

ALTERNATE PAIRINGS

Tempranillo from South America

Reds from Ribeira Sacra in Galicia

Dry reds from the Douro Valley in Portugal

APPROPRIATE DESSERT WINE

Sherry, from southern Spain

RIOJA

Spain's oldest and most famous wine region, Rioja, is credited with being the country's first growing area to draw interest from those serious about wine... even the Bordelaise. Rioja is close to France, and throughout its winemaking history has shared a strong connection with Bordeaux. In 1780, Manuel Quintano, a winemaker from Rioja, adopted the Bordelaise method of aging wine in oak barrels. Soon other Rioja winemakers adopted French techniques and sold their wine to the French, particularly in the mid-1800s when powdery mildew and the phylloxera louse nearly destroyed Bordeaux's wine production.

Rioja is known principally as a red wine region, and, similar to Bordeaux, the wines are usually a blend of grapes. Tempranillo is the predominant variety in all of the best red wines, and is blended with Garnacha (Grenache), Mazuelo (Carignan) and Graciano. Rioja has a tradition of extensive barrel and bottle aging, more so than any other wine region in the world. The result is a soft texture, an orange-ish/brick red color and an evolved flavor profile due to gradual oxidation that takes place in the barrel. This practice began in the eighteenth century, and while modern

tastes have shifted towards bigger, fresher and more extracted wine, extended barrel aging is still in use today, but to a lesser extent. The white wines of Rioja were also made following the oak-aging tradition, giving them a full-bodied, oxidative, Sherry-like quality. Today, more modern winemaking methods complement the traditional style, giving Rioja whites a wide range of styles. Viura (also known as Macabeo) is the main grape, but Malvasía is also used to make varietal wines and for blending.

Located in the northern part of Spain, Rioja is a large region that follows a 75-mile stretch of the Ebro River, with vines covering about 123,000 acres. Sitting on a vast plateau at 1,500 feet above sea level, Rioja is divided into three viticultural areas characterized by different terroirs, resulting in distinctly different styles of wine.

Rioja Alta is located west of Logroño between Alavesa in the north and Rioja Baja in the south. Alta is the most famous of the three regions, with higher-elevation vineyards and soil rich in chalk and iron, lending the grapes a higher natural acidity and thicker skin, making them excellent prospects for aging. Alta wines are firmer, darker and richer than those from the other two regions. The winemaking city of Haro is located here and is the cultural center of the region.

Rioja Alavesa is broken into two sections, both of which extend from the north shore of the Ebro River up into Basque country, making it culturally quite different from its neighboring zones. Alavesa wines are described as delicate, perfumed and fruit-forward; the best come from clay- and limestone-rich vineyard sites adjacent to the Sierra Cantabria Mountains.

Rioja Baja is the southernmost part of Rioja, starting at Logroño and heading south. Overall, the vineyard sites are at lower elevations and Garnacha grows well here. The vineyards in the hillsides, responsible for the zone's best wines, are at higher elevations and planted in calcareous clay soils. Despite good sites and good wines, Baja's wines are generally characterized as thicker and less elegant than wines from the other zones, though they can offer more immediate drinking and good value.

The finest red wines from Rioja enjoy a loyal following, though the number of enthusiasts dwindles each year as greater critical acclaim is heaped upon wines featuring bigger and bolder flavors. In contrast, properly aged Rioja is more akin to Burgundy in its nuance and detail than to Bordeaux's power and structure. This soft, round style of wine forms a natural pair with local cuisine emphasizing quality of ingredients and simplicity in preparation. The area is home to some of Spain's finest produce, excellent lamb and chorizo sausage, and is not far removed from the seafood of the coast. This diversity of ingredients welcomes all styles of Rioja, be it red, white or *rosado*, at the dinner table.

MAJOR WHITE GRAPES:

Viura (Macabeo)

Malvasía

MAJOR RED GRAPES:

Tempranillo

Garnacha

Mazuelo (Cariñena)

Graciano

NOTEWORTHY SUB-REGIONS:

Rioja Baja

Rioja Alavesa

Rioja Alta

Spain is known for its leisurely approach to mealtime, so the Rioja Burger is a simple recipe that allows you to relax with your dinner guests and enjoy a selection of white and rosado Rioja wines prior to cooking. This scrumptious lamb burger gets topped with Camerano or Manchego cheese along with a purée of roasted red peppers and artichoke hearts. The eggplant and asparagus side dish is served tapas-style: on wooden skewers, referred to as banderillas, named after the barbed sticks used in bullfighting.

RECOMMENDED COOKING METHOD: *Grill*   YIELDS: *4 servings*

BURGER INGREDIENTS:

1 ¼ lbs ground lamb

¼ cup finely chopped red bell pepper

2 cloves minced garlic

½ tsp paprika

1 tsp salt

ROASTED RED PEPPER & ARTICHOKE SPREAD:

½ cup lightly chopped roasted red bell peppers

¼ cup artichoke hearts, packed in oil

2 tsp red wine vinegar

¼ tsp salt

Breadcrumbs, as needed

ASSEMBLE WITH:

4 burger buns, split

Roasted red bell pepper and artichoke spread

Camerano or Manchego cheese slices

Romaine lettuce

SIDE DISH EGGPLANT AND ASPARAGUS BANDERILLAS:

1 medium eggplant

1 bunch asparagus

2 tbsp olive oil

1 tsp salt, plus ½ tsp

About 12 wooden skewers

TO PREPARE

1. **Make roasted red pepper and artichoke spread** - Combine red peppers, artichoke hearts, red wine vinegar and salt in a food processor. Pulse until smooth. Purée should be fairly thick. If it isn't, drain off excess liquid or add breadcrumbs as needed to create a texture that won't ooze off of the burger.

2. **Prep eggplant and asparagus banderillas** - Soak skewers in water for at least 15 minutes.

Cut asparagus into 1-inch pieces, and blanch in a saucepan of boiling water for about 1 minute. Drain and submerge in an ice bath to stop the cooking. Quarter the eggplant, and cut into 1-inch thick slices. Spread eggplant out on paper towels and sprinkle with ½ teaspoon of salt to draw out as much moisture and bitterness as possible. Wait at least 10 minutes, then rinse. Toss eggplant and asparagus in olive oil and 1 teaspoon of salt. Assemble on skewers and set aside.

3. **Combine burger ingredients** - Gently mix lamb, red bell pepper, garlic, paprika and salt in a mixing bowl. Form burgers and set aside.

4. **Gather buns and toppings, set aside.**

COOK & SERVE

1. **Heat grill to 400°.**

2. **Grill burgers and *banderillas*** - Grill burgers 3 to 4 minutes per side, or until cooked to preferred doneness. Add Camerano or Manchego during final minute of cooking. At the same time, grill the eggplant and asparagus skewers until asparagus is soft and lightly charred.

3. **Serve, topping burgers with romaine lettuce and red pepper artichoke spread.**

TRADITIONAL PAIRINGS

Rioja DOCa:

Rosé: Made primarily from Tempranillo and Garnacha, *rosado* from Rioja is relatively easy to find when the new rosés start showing up at your local wine shop each Spring. A well-aged, high-quality Rioja rosado would also make a nice match.

Red: Reds are usually a blend of a large percentage of Tempranillo, a bit of Garnacha and much smaller amounts of Graciano and Mazuelo.

Don't rule out sangria, which is made with a bottle of fruity, young Rioja, sliced fruits, a sweetener, brandy and carbonated water.

ALTERNATE PAIRINGS

Aged red Bordeaux

Reds from nearby Ribera Del Duero, Navarra, Campo de Borja and Calatayud

Rosé from Tavel in France's Rhône Valley

APPROPRIATE DESSERT WINE

Given the relationship between Rioja and Bordeaux, Sauternes would be a good way to follow up the Rioja burger.

PRIORAT

A miraculous vision brought the first Carthusian monks to this land in the twelfth century. The region was named *Priorato* by locals for the abundance of small, remote priories that once dotted the landscape, where monks lived a life of isolation and viticultural toil. Eight hundred years later, opportunity and ambition brought a wealth of talented winemakers to this corner of Spain as the twentieth century drew to a close. The wilderness of Tarragona, 60 miles south of Barcelona, contains distinct natural advantages. Discerning winemakers understood the possibilities of Priorat's otherworldly terrain and widespread old-vine plantings. Luckily for them, until very recently Priorat was enough of a viticultural hinterland to allow ambitious winemakers to piece together estates containing parcels of century-old vines. René Barbier, the first who saw the potential of this underutilized terroir, laid the foundation for a renaissance in the 1980s. By the early '90s he and four fellow visionaries were producing a series of "Clos" wines that would catapult Priorat into the upper echelon of Spanish wines: Barbier's own Clos Mogador, Alvaro Palacios' Clos Dofí (now Finca Dofí), Daphne Glorian's Clos Erasmus, Carles Pastrana's Clos de l'Obac and José Luis Perez's Clos Martinet.

Today, the Priorat, barely a pinpoint on Spain's map, has made it: without argument it is among the top DOs for red wine in Spain. Accolades - and more winemakers - have come flooding in, thanks to the work of Barbier and friends. Priorat is one of three regions in Spain, along with Rioja and Ribera Del Duero, to receive the top-tier DOCa designation. Steep cliffs of terraced vines made the area a sleeping giant for red wine, forged by nature with the components for greatness. Vineyards rise from 300 to 2,000 feet above sea level in the best mesoclimates of Priorat. Slate-dominated soils, known locally as *llicorella*, force grapevines to send roots deep into the earth in search of sustenance. The slate traps what little rain falls in Priorat and provides scant but adequate nourishment for vines forced to eke out existence in this harsh climate. Yields are low due to the aforementioned conditions, and because of the natural vigor-limiting properties of extremely old vines. These factors combine to produce deeply flavorful grapes.

White wine production is miniscule in Priorat, taking up less than five percent of the region's precious vineyard space. Garnacha Blanca, the leading white grape, accounts for a whopping 2.5 percent of all plantings. Make no mistake about it; Priorat is most definitely red wine country. Modernly-styled Priorat wines are dark, dense and concentrated, typically finished off with a judicious touch of oak that fades into the background by the time the wine has reached its prime drinking window. Other times, the wines are clearly akin to those rustic, unpolished wines made from the same grapes in the Languedoc-Roussillon in southern France, about a four-hour drive away. Garnacha and Cariñena lead the way in terms of planted acres, followed by Cabernet Sauvignon, Syrah and, to a lesser extent, Merlot. Aromas and flavors of blueberry, cassis, blackberry and cherry fruit are often prominent in the marquee red wines of this land.

The cuisine of Catalonia is more closely related to that of Mediterranean France than it is to any other part of Spain. Pork, poultry, lamb, veal and various forms of seafood are commonly found in the Catalan kitchen. Rice, nuts and fresh vegetables are all popular accompaniments to these staples, and a healthy dose of garlic is often present. Hearty Catalan dishes are ideally matched with a bottle or two of Priorat red to be enjoyed with friends over the course of a relaxed, unhurried evening.

MAJOR WHITE GRAPES:

Garnacha Blanca

Macabeo

MAJOR RED GRAPES:

Garnacha

Cariñena

Syrah

Cabernet Sauvignon

Merlot

The Priorat Burger combines two local specialties: a veal dish called fricandó de vedella, a Catalan mainstay for hundreds of years, and romesco sauce, made with roasted tomatoes and hazelnuts or almonds. Making either one of these recipes on its own is a time-consuming process, so in combining the two I have scaled down the ingredient list and simplified the cooking process. The Priorat Burger is served with the traditional side dish for fricandó de vedella, a spinach salad with raisins and pine nuts.

RECOMMENDED COOKING METHOD: *Grill*   YIELDS: *4 servings*

BURGER INGREDIENTS:

1 ¼ lbs ground veal

1 medium carrot, peeled and cut into 1-inch pieces

½ cup whole hazelnuts or almonds

¼ cup fresh parsley

1 tsp salt

¼ tsp ground black pepper

ROMESCO SAUCE:

14 oz can diced tomatoes, well drained

2 tbsp red wine vinegar

1 - 2 cloves minced garlic

1 cup whole hazelnuts or almonds

1 ½ tsp chili powder or sweet paprika

1 tsp salt

2 tbsp olive oil

SAUTÉED PORCINI MUSHROOMS:

4 oz fresh porcini mushrooms or 1 oz dried

2 tbsp butter

Pinch salt

ASSEMBLE WITH:

4 burger buns, split

Garrotxa cheese slices (or other semi-firm aged goat cheese)

Romesco sauce

Sautéed porcini mushrooms

SIDE DISH WILTED CATALAN SPINACH SALAD:

6 cups spinach

½ cup raisins

2 tbsp pine nuts

1 clove garlic, thinly sliced

1 tbsp red wine vinegar

3 tbsp olive oil

Salt and pepper to taste

TO PREPARE

1. If dried, rehydrate porcini in a bowl of warm water for 30 minutes. Drain and set aside.

2. **Combine burger ingredients** - Combine carrot, ½ cup hazelnuts and parsley in a small food processor and pulse to a fine texture. Gently combine with veal, salt and pepper in a large mixing bowl. Form burgers and set aside.

3. Gather buns and toppings, set aside. Gather wilted spinach salad ingredients; salad should be prepared while the burgers are cooking and/or resting.

COOK & SERVE

1. **Sauté porcini mushrooms** - Place a large sauté pan on medium-high heat with 2 tablespoons butter. Add porcini and stir occasionally until lightly browned. Sprinkle with salt and stir. Remove from pan and set aside.

2. **Make romesco sauce** - Pulse hazelnuts in food processor until ground to a powder. Heat olive oil in a sauté pan over medium heat. Add hazelnuts, garlic and chili powder to pan and sauté 1 minute. Drain tomatoes and pulse in food processor. Add tomatoes to sauté pan along with vinegar and salt. Reduce heat to low and simmer until sauce has thickened, about 20 minutes.

3. **Heat grill to 400°.**

4. **Grill burgers 3 to 4 minutes per side, or until cooked to preferred doneness. Add Garrotxa during final minute of cooking.**

5. **Assemble salad** - Sauté garlic in a pan with 3 tablespoons of olive oil set over low heat. At the first signs of browning, add raisins and pine nuts. Cook until raisins plump up and lighten in color. Remove from heat and add red wine vinegar and spinach. Toss gently to wilt spinach and coat with olive oil. Season to taste with salt and pepper.

6. **Serve, topping burgers with porcini and romesco sauce.**

TRADITIONAL PAIRINGS

Priorat DOCa:

White: Full-bodied whites produced from Garnacha Blanca, Macabeo and a handful of other white grapes that play a small role in the area.

Rosé: *Rosado* from Priorat is a delicious rarity that would be right at home with this recipe. They are crafted from the red grapes listed below.

Red: Reds are composed of Garnacha, Cariñena and/or Cabernet Sauvignon, often with some Syrah or Merlot rounding out the blend.

ALTERNATE PAIRINGS

Reds from surrounding Montsant, made from a similar selection of grapes

Reds from Jumilla and Yecla, down the coast from Priorat

Reds from France's Roussillon

APPROPRIATE DESSERT WINE

While rare, it is possible to find some late-harvest Garnacha that's similar in flavor profile to Banyuls from France. In the event that you can't find a dessert wine from Priorat, seek out Banyuls as an alternative.

PENEDÈS

Penedès is at the center of Catalonia, a large region of Northeastern Spain whose ambassador to the outside world has long been the bustling and culturally-rich port city of Barcelona. Though part of Spain, Catalonia has enjoyed a substantial power of self-governance and protection of its language and distinct Catalan identity since the waning years of the Franco era in the early- to mid-1970s.

Any discussion of Catalonia's culture must mention its remarkable cuisine, as it has become one of the great gastronomic capitals of Europe since the middle of the last century. The region is blessed with an abundance of flavorful ingredients that have fueled a distinctive and top-quality culinary tradition stretching back for generations. Even the simple food is outstanding here. Chefs who grew up eating regional specialties incorporated their vibrance and unique character into their work, even if the methods they employed were miles from traditional, rustic cooking techniques. For the culinarily adventurous, Catalonia offers the groundbreaking work of Ferran Adrià and his disciples of deconstructivist molecular gastronomy.

Seafood is at the center of all this, not surprising given Catalonia's lengthy history as a prominent maritime trading port. The resulting exposure to foreign cultures, combined with the frequent conquests this region endured over the course of millennia, brought innumerable ingredients and culinary complexity to the kitchens of Penedès. Today, asparagus, artichokes, olives, wild mushrooms and peppers are all staples of Catalan cooking. A fantastic selection of cheeses is made here as well. For a creative cook, Penedès has it all.

Winemaking in Penedès dates back some 2,500 years, with numerous red varieties brought over by the Greeks. Over time, white wine production slowly overtook that of red. By the sixth century, its renowned location made Penedès one of the early powerhouses of wine production in the Mediterranean. Today, grapes indigenous to all parts of Europe are grown in Penedès, making it one of Spain's most viticulturally varied winegrowing regions. This, coupled with its proximity to Barcelona, has enabled the region's wine industry to flourish again. To understand its diversity, you really need to see Penedès as a series of hillside vineyards, each specializing in different areas of wine production.

PENEDÈS

Grown throughout the region's lower slopes, Xarel-lo, Macabeo and Parellada are the typical components of Cava production. These sparklers are made in the same exacting, high-quality method as Champagne, via a secondary fermentation that takes place in the bottle, and sometimes feature the traditional Champagne grapes Chardonnay and Pinot Noir. It often lacks the finesse of its French counterpart, but Cava represents a far more affordable choice for pre-dinner festivities and matches well with much of Catalan's Mediterranean cuisine. It is also viewed in a different light, as a beverage intended for everyday consumption. While Cava production takes place in other areas of Spain, Penedès is far and away the quality and quantity leader.

Although Cava has been produced in Penedès since the 1800s, the area has been producing still wines far longer. The same varieties used for Cava find their way into the fresh and brisk still whites that are equally at home with the coast's seafood. Whether made into varietal wines or blended for greater complexity, oak influence is minimal, acidity is generally high and the best wines can be surprisingly Chablis-like.

Higher up the slopes in Penedès, Merlot, Tempranillo (known locally as Ull de Llebre) and Cabernet Sauvignon are the grapes of choice for the small amount of red wine that is produced here. These wines can be quite rich and concentrated, often spending some time in oak. On the very upper slopes, where vineyard sites can reach well beyond 2,000 feet above sea level, cool-climate-loving Gewürztraminer, Riesling, Chardonnay, Pinot Noir and a handful of other varieties do extremely well, presenting a broad choice of flavors to pair with the adventurous dishes coming out of Catalonia's top kitchens. In time, we in the United States are sure to see more of these esoteric gems to pair with our own favorite meals.

MAJOR WHITE GRAPES:

Xarel-lo

Macabeo

Parellada

Chardonnay

MAJOR RED GRAPES:

Garnacha

Tempranillo

Cabernet Sauvignon

NOTEWORTHY SUB-REGIONS:

Alt Penedès

Penedès Central

Baix Penedès

PENEDÈS

Spain's sparkling Cava is a delicious pair with this combo of duck, chicken, blue cheese and sautéed pear. I never need an excuse to open up a bottle of bubbly, but if you use this delicious burger as your reason for popping the cork I'm sure you'll be happy with your decision. And what goes great with sparkling wine? More sparkling wine, of course! Feel free to try this with a white and a rosado Cava, or with the equally enjoyable still white wines of Penedès.

RECOMMENDED COOKING METHOD: *Cast iron pan*   YIELDS: *4 servings*

BURGER INGREDIENTS:

¾ lb finely chopped duck (2 duck breasts, with skin and fat)

½ lb ground chicken, preferably dark meat

⅓ cup raisins

⅓ cup pine nuts

1 tsp salt

Breadcrumbs as needed

SIMPLIFIED ALLIOLI:

1 clove minced garlic

¼ cup mayonnaise

1 tsp olive oil

2 tsp lemon juice

¼ tsp salt

SAUTÉED PEARS:

One large brown pear, sliced ⅛-inch thick, core removed

1 tbsp butter

Squirt of lemon juice

ASSEMBLE WITH:

4 burger buns, split

Blue cheese slices or crumbles

Sautéed pears

Allioli

SIDE DISH CATALAN BAKED BEANS:

2 15-oz cans white beans (cannellini or great northern), drained and rinsed

1 15-oz can diced tomatoes

8 slices serrano ham (or prosciutto), roughly chopped

2 tbsp olive oil

2 cloves minced garlic

½ tsp salt

TO PREPARE

1. **Make allioli** - Combine mayonnaise, garlic, olive oil, lemon juice and salt in a mixing bowl and whisk thoroughly. Refrigerate until serving.

2. **Combine burger ingredients** - Place raisins and pine nuts in a food processor and grind to a paste. Transfer to a large mixing bowl. Cut duck breasts into 1-inch cubes and place in the food processor. Pulse several times to achieve desired texture. Transfer to mixing bowl with raisin-pine nut mixture and add chicken, breadcrumbs and salt. Mix gently. Form burgers and set aside.

3. **Gather buns and toppings, set aside.**

COOK & SERVE

1. **Make Catalan baked beans** - In a large saucepan, warm olive oil over high heat. Add serrano ham and cook until crispy. Remove and set aside, leaving the oil in the pan. Add white beans and garlic to saucepan and cook until beans start to brown slightly. Add tomatoes and salt. Stir, and reduce heat to medium-low. Cook until liquid has reduced to a sauce consistency. Add serrano ham and stir.

2. **Sauté pears** - Melt butter in sauté pan set over medium-high heat. Add pear slices and a squirt of lemon juice and cook 30 seconds per side, until pears just barely soften and brown slightly. Remove from pan and set aside.

3. Preheat a large cast iron pan or skillet on a 375° grill or on a stovetop burner set to medium-high heat. Drizzle the pan with vegetable oil just before adding burgers.

4. Cook burgers 4 minutes per side, or until cooked to preferred doneness.

5. Serve, topping burgers with blue cheese, pear slices and allioli.

PENEDÈS

TRADITIONAL PAIRINGS

Sparkling: Cava, made in the Traditional Method, primarily from Xarel-lo, Parellada, Macabeo and Chardonnay. *Rosado* (rosé) Cava is made from various red grapes, particularly Pinot Noir.

White: Still whites are typically composed of Xarel-lo and Macabeo, though Muscat, Chardonnay and Riesling are also used.

ALTERNATE PAIRINGS

Champagne and other great sparkling wines from around the world

Whites from Rueda, Rioja, the Basque Country and elsewhere in Spain

White Burgundy, particularly Chablis

APPROPRIATE DESSERT WINE

Rivesaltes, from nearby Languedoc-Roussillon in France, the best of which are made from the Muscat grape.

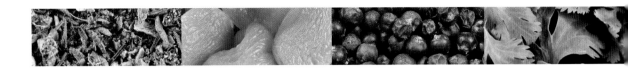

PORTUGAL'S governing body which oversees wine production is the Denominação de Origem Controlada (DOC). For the most part, wines are labeled according to place-name, rather than the grape(s) used to make the wine, though it is not uncommon to find the variety(s) listed on the back label. Vinho Regional and Vinho de Mesa are classifications for Portuguese wines which do not meet the standards required for Denominação de Origem Controlada status.

GERMAN wine labels feature long names that rarely roll off the tongue, but the silver lining is that these labels divulge far more information than most other European wine labels, often including a village and vineyard source. Wines classified as Qualitätswein bestimmter Anbaugebiete (QbA) offer good everyday drinking, while Prädikatswein covers the top wines and categorizes them according to harvest date. Wines made from the earliest harvested grapes of the vintage are labeled as Kabinett and tend to be made in an off-dry style. Spätlese and Auslese wines are made from grapes harvested after those in Kabinetts, and a moderate amount of sweetness is to be expected. Beerenauslese, Trockenbeerenauslese and Eiswein are made from grapes with successively later harvest dates and will always have significant sweetness.

AUSTRIAN wines are classified in a virtually identical manner as those from Germany, though prädikat terms, such as Kabinett, Spätlese and Auslese, are rarely listed on a label. The biggest stylistic difference between German and Austrian wines is that, generally speaking, Austria's wines are fermented to dryness.

GREECE'S wine production is currently divided into four categories, as determined by the Central Committee for the Protection of Wine Production. Onomasia Proelefseos Anotéras Piotitos (OPAP) is reserved for the best dry wines in Greece, while Onomasia Proelefseos Eleghomeni (OPE) covers the country's best sweet wines. Both are similar to France's AOC designation. Topikos Inos is roughly the same as France's Vin de Pays, while Epitrapezios Inos is applied to simple table wines.

PORTUGAL

For much of the seventeenth and eighteenth centuries, the British just could not seem to stop fighting the French. This, of course, caused a major trade dilemma because the British had absolutely no desire to quit drinking, and the French were their primary source for wine since their own little island was too cold for growing quality wine grapes. In a bid to diversify their supply, the British drafted a trade treaty with Portugal in 1703 that would form the foundation of a centuries-long affinity for the country's sweet wines. In exchange for a ban on any tariffs on U.K. textiles, the British agreed to ban any tax on Portuguese alcohol. And what did they import? Mainly reds from the Douro Valley, revved up with brandy – a concoction that became known as Port. Some say brandy fortification was added to make Port ready for its arduous transoceanic voyage. It is equally plausible that the booze was intended to maintain residual sugar levels and mask the sometimes less-than-elegant nature of the original wine. Even today, a young Douro red from the wrong cellar can be pretty daunting, rough stuff.

The British basically took over the Portuguese wine industry. It became stable and profitable under the control of companies with very un-Portuguese names like Graham's, Taylor Fladgate and Gould Campbell. As with many wine regions across Europe, the industry was structured to keep peasant farmers farming, and British merchants and their local assistants in charge of the wine making, wine selling and profit reaping. In Portugal the crucial piece of legislation, on the books until 1986, was that all wine made in the Douro had to be shipped in bulk to Vila Nova de Gaia for bottling, a town some sixty miles away. No small-scale farmer could afford to maintain a separate bottling and shipping facility so far from their vines, so wines made by locals remained shut out of the export market. As a result, quality Port production is still very much dominated by large shippers. Warre's, Dow's, Graham's, Fonseca and Taylor Fladgate all jostle for the top of the ladder of vintage Port quality. Single Quinta (vineyard) Ports are starting to see the light of day, providing an opportunity to experience a more site-specific bit of Portuguese terroir.

Often overlooked in the dessert wine discussion, Madeira is another uniquely Portuguese product. Made on the island of Madeira, the wine is heated in attics or in specially designed oven-like *estufagems*.

This mimics the effects of this fortified beverage's voyage across the ocean, which literally cooked it as it passed through the equator. The resulting wine is capable of displaying a wide range of flavors, from orange zest and dried fruits to toffee and cocoa.

The Douro, Portugal's most important appellation, is a hot, steep and rocky place, a region that unsurprisingly produces some of the brawniest red wines in Europe. Indigenous grape varieties are abundant here, most significantly Touriga Nacional, but also Tinta Barroca and Tinta Francisca among many, many others. Along with the nearby regions of Dão and Bairrada, the Douro is responsible for most of the top-quality red and fortified Portuguese wines to be consumed outside of Portugal.

The quality of Portugal's dry red wine production has made great strides recently, and more of these wines are finding their way to the American market each year. Light-bodied reds are reminiscent of young, inexpensive Rioja: fruity, soft on the palate and easy drinking. More serious examples are packed with tannin and reward those who lay their bottles down for several years or more.

In Portugal's far north, farmers in the Minho region produce the country's most popular white wine: Vinho Verde. Light, refreshing, low in alcohol and slightly sparkling, Vinho Verde is the quintessential summertime wine. It can be the perfect fit on a hot day with a first course of fresh seafood, at a sidewalk café in Lisbon or at your favorite beach. When they are Alvarinho-based versions from the subregion of Monção, and when the slight fizz is the natural by-product of fermentation rather than pumped-in carbon dioxide, Vinho Verde can rightfully claim a place among the great thirst-quenching summer wines of all time.

MAJOR WHITE GRAPES:

Alvarinho

Verdelho

Malvasia Fina

Sercial

Loureiro

Trajadura

MAJOR RED GRAPES:

Touriga Nacional

Tinta Roriz

Aragonêz

Tinta Cão

NOTEWORTHY SUB-REGIONS:

Douro

Dão

Vinho Verde

Alentejo

Madeira

PORTUGAL

The Portugal Burger is a prime example of delving deeper than the surface of a country's culinary identity to create a recipe. Omnipresent bacalhao, or salt cod, would be the logical starting ingredient for this recipe, but the delicate texture of this flaky white fish isn't ideal for creating a burger patty. Instead, the Portugal Burger is made with chicken, which is also more accepting of the range of Portugal's dry wines, from spritzy Vinho Verde to the plethora of reds now gaining prominence in the US.

RECOMMENDED COOKING METHOD: *Cast iron pan*   YIELDS: *4 servings*

BURGER INGREDIENTS:

1 ½ lbs ground chicken

¼ cup finely chopped cilantro

2 cloves minced garlic

2 tsp ground coriander

1 tsp paprika

1 tsp salt

½ tsp ground black pepper

Breadcrumbs as needed

CILANTRO COLESLAW:

1 cup coarsely grated cabbage

¼ cup coarsely grated carrot

¼ cup finely chopped cilantro

2 tbsp mayonnaise

1 tsp lemon juice

Salt and pepper to taste

ASSEMBLE WITH:

4 burger buns, split

Tomato slices

Queijo da Serra or Brie cheese

Cilantro coleslaw

SAFFRON RICE WITH CHOURIÇO:

1 ½ cups uncooked white rice

2 cups water

2 bay leaves

Pinch saffron

8 oz chouriço (chorizo) or linguiça, chopped

1 tsp ground coriander

⅓ cup corn kernels (drained/thawed, if frozen)

1 tbsp tomato paste

2 tbsp olive oil

2 tbsp white wine vinegar

TO PREPARE

1. **Make cilantro coleslaw** - Combine cabbage, carrot, cilantro, mayonnaise and lemon juice and mix thoroughly. Add salt and pepper to taste.

2. **Combine burger ingredients** - Gently mix chicken, cilantro, garlic, coriander, paprika, salt and pepper in a large mixing bowl. Add breadcrumbs only as needed, until chicken no longer sticks to your hands while mixing. Form burgers and set aside.

3. **Gather buns and toppings, set aside.**

COOK & SERVE

1. **Make saffron rice with chouriço** - Bring two cups of water to a boil. Add rice and bay leaves and reduce heat to medium. When most of the moisture has been absorbed, approximately 15 to 20 minutes, add the saffron and stir. Continue to cook until rice is soft, about 3 more minutes. Meanwhile, in a large saucepan, sauté the chouriço over medium-high heat until lightly browned. Add corn, coriander and tomato paste. Continue cooking until chouriço is fully browned. Add rice to chouriço, leaving the bay leaves in as garnish. Add olive oil and white wine vinegar and stir. Remove from heat and cover.

2. **Preheat a large cast iron pan on a 375° grill or on a stovetop burner set to medium-high heat. Drizzle the pan with vegetable oil just before adding burgers.**

3. **Cook burgers 3 to 4 minutes per side, or until cooked to preferred doneness.**

4. **Serve, topping burgers with tomato, cilantro coleslaw and Queijo da Serra or Brie.**

PORTUGAL

	Noteworthy DOCs:	*Grape(s):*
White:	Vinho Verde	Alvarinho, Arinto, Loureiro, Trajadura
	Dão	Encruzado, Bical, Sercial, Verdelho, Malvasia Fina
	Bairrada	Fernão Pires, Arinto
	Alentejo	Ropier, Antão Vaz, Arinto
	Estremadura	Arinto, Fernão Pires
Red:	Light-bodied Portuguese reds	

White or rosé Txakoli, from the Basque region of Spain

Verdelho from Australia

Light, fruity reds such as Beaujolais and inexpensive Rioja

Easily one of the world's greatest dessert wines, Port is the obvious choice,
but don't forget Madeira for a change of pace.

GERMANY

Great German white wine stands alone for many wine lovers. Terroir may be a French word and concept, but sip a glass of Riesling made from grapes grown along the steep slate hillsides of southwestern Germany and the obvious connection between the vertigo-inducing source and the beautiful end product is clear. These special hills are given definition by innumerable waving lines of vines, and offer tourists with a combined love of wine and the outdoors hundreds of kilometers of unblemished landscape to traverse. The Germans love to bike, and who wouldn't with all this beauty in their backyard?

The Mosel is a disarmingly bucolic land, and it's not surprising that wines made in this winding river valley are fresh, spring-like and lively. They charm drinkers with green apple aromas and offer fruit that can seem weightless, even when tethered to a liquid often containing abundant grape sugars. The key is acidity, and here it cuts cleanly through the wine to accent what is often nuanced flavor. Preferred vineyard locations cross from one side of the river to the other as the Mosel bends, in order to catch precious sunlight in this cool corner of northern Europe. Each twist in the river or dip in the hillside presents a case study in Mosel terroir. Similar to Burgundy in eastern France, the fractured nature of vine ownership excites wine collectors as it allows for direct study of the relative influence of man and nature in the ultimate quality of wine. A wine lover can sit with several different wines made from the same vineyard, in the same year, from highly regarded producers, and scrutinize the fingerprint of these estates' talented winemakers. Sun, soil, precipitation; all variables the same - save for one.

A first view of the Rheingau can be altogether different. Overlooking the arcs of vines and the wide Rhein River, wines here ascend, hitting notes of purity and clarity. Refinement is a hard quality to articulate, but an easy one to experience. This is the classic heart of German viticulture. The wines of nearby Mosel may be as good, but they are also altogether different. Rheingau Riesling is often described as racy: closer to the mark for the best wines would be words like "soaring" or "majestic." The estates that create these high-wire wines produce a small number of bottles per vintage, so don't hesitate to grab one when afforded the opportunity.

Just south of the Rheingau, the Rheinhessen is a difficult area to organize. It is large and full of relatively undifferentiated towns whose names all tend to end with "heim." Because wine towns are widely scattered, the growers who are reshaping the region are often working in isolation from each other. Determined young winemakers are earning a degree of recognition for often good, sometimes great Riesling, particularly in the villages of Weinheim, Westhofen, Siefersheim and Oppenheim.

To the west of the Rheinhessen lies the Nahe region. Its wines bear a resemblance to those of the Mosel, though with a bigger personality and greater richness. The best producers in the Nahe - names like Dönnhoff, Diel and Emrich-Schönleber - are able to maintain the acidity required to achieve perfect balance in this opulent style. The region has a diversity of soils that allows winemakers to coax wonderful expression from an assortment of grape varieties, including Riesling, Müller-Thurgau and Silvaner.

Pfalz displays a penchant for dry whites, a style mastered at the Müller-Catoir estate. The wines somehow convey the freshest summer peach aroma any drinker could dream of, with a finish as fine, dry and stony as a perfect Sancerre. Pfalz, a land close to the French border, succeeds with dry whites more often than most other German regions. Scheurebe and Rieslaner, two quality German grapes that exist on the commercial periphery, find a sympathetic homeland in the Pfalz.

Riesling's popularity has been on the decline for some time in the United States, as wine drinkers have been scolded for enjoying sweet wines. While there are many cloying, poorly made, downright nasty sweet wines on the market, it's unfair to cast the entire category aside, particularly when it comes to German Riesling. These wines can offer tremendous bang for the buck, and are incredibly food-friendly when paired correctly. When in doubt, just add pork.

MAJOR WHITE GRAPES:

Riesling

Müller-Thurgau

Silvaner

Gewürztraminer

MAJOR RED GRAPES:

Spätburgunder
(Pinot Noir)

Dornfelder

NOTEWORTHY SUB-REGIONS:

Mosel

Rheingau

Rheinhessen

Pfalz

Nahe

GERMANY

The Germany Burger is inspired very loosely by a dish called Schlesisches Himmelreich, or Silesian pork, combining pork and apricots to create a perfect compliment to the country's fabulous Rieslings, from bone-dry trockens to the finest Spätlese and Auslese. Save the Trockenbeerenauslese and Eiswein for dessert. The side dish takes the traditional recipe for German-style potato salad and turns it into a delicious rendition of mashed potatoes.

RECOMMENDED COOKING METHOD: *Grill*   YIELDS: *4 servings*

BURGER INGREDIENTS:

1 ¼ lbs ground pork

⅓ cup finely chopped dried apricots

2 tsp finely chopped marjoram

2 tsp ground cardamom

1 tsp salt

ASSEMBLE WITH:

4 burger buns, split

Thinly sliced cabbage

Emmenthaler cheese slices

4 – 8 slices bacon

German mustard (mild, sweet or hot)

SIDE DISH GERMAN-STYLE
MASHED POTATOES:

1 ½ lbs red potatoes

3 slices bacon, roughly chopped

Bacon drippings

2 tbsp German-style mustard

¼ cup thinly sliced green onions

2 tbsp white wine vinegar

¼ cup heavy cream

Salt and pepper to taste

TO PREPARE

1. **Combine burger ingredients** - Gently mix pork, apricots, marjoram, cardamom and salt in a large mixing bowl. Form burgers and set aside.

2. **Gather buns and toppings, set aside.**

COOK & SERVE

1. **Make German-style mashed potatoes** - Rinse potatoes and cut into 1-inch chunks. Fill a large pot with cold water and 1 tablespoon of salt. Add potatoes and bring to a boil, then simmer approximately 10 minutes.

While potatoes are cooking, sauté roughly chopped bacon over medium heat.

Potatoes are done when you can pierce them with a knife without resistance. Drain and return to low-medium heat. Add bacon and drippings, vinegar, mustard and heavy cream and mash slightly. Add salt and pepper to taste. Garnish with sliced green onions. Remove from heat.

2. **Cook bacon for burgers - Cook 1 to 2 slices per burger in large sauté pan.**

3. **Heat grill to 400˚.**

4. Grill burgers 3 to 4 minutes per side, or until cooked to preferred doneness. Add Emmenthaler during the final minute of cooking.

5. Serve, topping burgers with cabbage, bacon and a dollop of your preferred mustard.

GERMANY

Varietally-labeled wines:

Sparkling: Sekt, made from Riesling, Pinot Blanc and Pinot Gris

White: Whites, ranging from dry to fairly sweet, labeled as trocken, halbtrocken, Kabinett, Spätlese or Auslese:

Riesling

Müller-Thurgau

Silvaner

Red: Spätburgunder (Pinot Noir)

Dornfelder

Riesling from Washington

Vouvray from the Loire Valley in France

Whites and reds from neighboring Austria

Beerenauslese, Trockenbeerenauslese or Eiswein, made mainly from Riesling

AUSTRIA

Austria's signature grape, Grüner Veltliner, is made into many different styles of wine. You'd expect as much from the country's most planted white grape, which covers nearly 50,000 acres, mostly around Vienna. Grüner Veltliner shares a strong connection with Austria's soil composition, so it's rarely grown abroad. Loess soil is common throughout the nation's prime viticultural areas and aids farmers greatly in their quest to grow fully ripe fruit in a cool continental climate. Loess is permeable to moisture, which allows rain to soak through the surface, making roots bore deeper underground. It's also very low in organic material and therefore naturally prevents vines from overproducing.

Limiting yields in the vineyard and stirring the lees, or yeast cells, during fermentation and aging makes for earthy, concentrated white wines. This treatment represents an older style that beautifully complements the country's rich cuisine. In America, these satisfying bottlings are currently less fashionable than a cleaner, lighter style of Grüner Veltliner, made at cool temperatures in stainless steel tanks. This crisp style is more than simply light and fruity. These wines are capable of great complexity with nuanced aromatics.

White pepper, lychee, peach and other stone fruit aromas are the foreground flavors of modern, clean and vibrant Grüner Veltliner. This trendy grape variety is a favorite of sommeliers as a match for fresh and spicy Asian dishes. Despite Grüner's recent ascent in popularity, Austria's wine as a whole is still a relative unknown to wine neophytes and aficionados alike.

While Grüner Veltliner is Austria's calling card, it's certainly not the only noteworthy grape in the region. Riesling attains great heights in both dry, mineral-driven wines with lively acidity, as well as some of the world's best dessert wines. St. Laurent, Zweigelt, Blaufrankisch and Blauburgunder (Pinot Noir) make surprisingly approachable light- to medium-bodied red wines, packed with silky red fruits and hints of spice. There's also the inevitable experimentation with fuller-bodied international varieties such as Cabernet Sauvignon, Merlot and Syrah.

The vineyards in the Kamptal region to the west of Vienna tend toward rocky, dry, sunny hillside sites with good drainage. Grapes harvested here become wines of a full, ripe texture. More fertile, calcareous vineyards closer to sea level can naturally add a fine, chalky minerality to the finished wines. This pronounced soil characteristic keeps Kamptaler wines from being one-dimensionally fruity. Tradition here involves deep, cold cellars where wines mature in old oak and acacia casks. The wines are not excessively flavored by this time in barrel, but rather become rounder, deeper and more interesting. The top vineyards in Kamptal have a recognizable voice across a span of vintages, and are among the most accessible and food-versatile wines from Austria.

Wagram is a region on the banks of the Danube northwest of Vienna. This area is also referred to as the Donauland, or Danube-land. It's just east of the Kamptal, and is one of Austria's premier wine-growing areas. The soils of Wagram give richness and spicy aromatics to Grüner Veltliner, Zweigelt and Blauburgunder.

Along the Danube in the Wachau region, rocky, terraced hillside vineyards offer perfect geology for heat retention and drainage, ideal conditions for producing amazing wine. Truly top-drawer stuff, or at least it can be. Less than 3,700 acres are planted in the region, nowhere near enough to provide wine for the legions of tourists, importers and locals seeking this special wine, so prices can be high. The potential is staggering. Grown in the right field, farmed by the right hands, these Grüner Veltliner- and Riesling-based wines can blow your mind. Addiction to Smaragd – the Wachau's top honor, named for the lizards that patrol the area's warmest vineyards – will cost you.

Kremstal used to be lumped together with neighboring Kamptal, but in recent years has gained recognition as a separate entity. Fans of white wines from neighboring Wachau should take note: stylistic similarities exist, and prices are almost always lower in Kremstal. The area is as warm as the Wachau, and many of its best farmers bottle wines that are worthy of several years of cellaring. Kremstal wines are often light, faintly herbal and as refreshing as cold spring water. Simply put, they taste good and they make you want to drink more.

MAJOR WHITE GRAPES:

Grüner Veltliner

Riesling

MAJOR RED GRAPES:

Zweigelt

St. Laurent

Blaufrankisch

Blauburgunder
(Pinot Noir)

NOTEWORTHY SUB-REGIONS:

Wachau

Kremstal

Kamptal

Wagram
(formerly Donauland)

Carnuntum

Burgenland

The Austria Burger uses some unusual ingredients, but after having this amazing burger you'll start using them more often. Juniper berries impart an herbal, piney quality, while horseradish adds some bite. Speck is tough to find, but can be replicated by rubbing prosciutto with ground juniper berries. The Liptauer cheese spread may look a little odd at first, but trust me, you'll start making it on its own as a pretzel dip while sipping on Austria's array of vastly under-appreciated wines.

RECOMMENDED COOKING METHOD: *Grill*   **YIELDS:** *4 servings*

BURGER INGREDIENTS:

1 ¼ lbs ground veal

⅓ cup finely chopped onion

2 tbsp finely chopped chives

1 tbsp finely chopped fresh marjoram

2 tsp grated horseradish

1 tsp ground juniper berries

½ tsp salt

LIPTAUER CHEESE SPREAD:

4 oz quark or cream cheese, room temperature

⅓ cup finely chopped onion

4 lightly chopped cornichons

2 tsp lightly chopped capers

1 tsp paprika

¼ tsp ground caraway seed

¼ tsp salt

ASSEMBLE WITH:

4 burger buns, split

Liptauer cheese spread

4 – 8 slices of speck, or Prosciutto rubbed with ground juniper berries

Lettuce

SIDE DISH GRILLED WHITE ASPARAGUS:

1 bunch white asparagus

1 tbsp olive oil

½ tsp salt

1 tbsp finely chopped chives

TO PREPARE

1. **Make Liptauer cheese spread** - In a medium mixing bowl, add quark or cream cheese, onion, cornichons, capers, paprika, caraway and salt. Mix well to combine and set aside.

2. **Combine burger ingredients** - Combine veal, juniper berries, onion, chives, marjoram, horseradish and salt. Gently form into burgers. Set aside.

3. **Prep asparagus** - Rinse and trim off the bottom ½ inch of the asparagus. Drizzle lightly with olive oil and sprinkle with salt.

4. **Gather buns and toppings, set aside.**

COOK & SERVE

1. **Heat grill to 400˚.**

2. **Grill or sauté speck/prosciutto** - Cook 1 to 2 slices of speck per burger. If you can't find speck, rub prosciutto with a dusting of ground juniper berries prior to cooking. Cook until lightly crispy.

3. **Grill burgers and asparagus** - Grill burgers 3 to 4 minutes per side, or until cooked to preferred doneness. Grill asparagus until soft, turning once during cooking.

4. **Serve, topping burgers with speck, Liptauer and lettuce. Garnish asparagus with chopped chives. Serve with a side of remaining Liptauer.**

AUSTRIA

Varietally-labeled wines:

Sparkling:	Sekt, Austria's sparkling wine, is made from numerous grapes, most often Grüner Veltliner and Riesling

White:

Grüner Veltliner

Riesling

Welschriesling

Scheurebe (Sämling 88)

Grauburgunder (Pinot Gris/Pinot Grigio)

International varieties: Chardonnay, Sauvignon Blanc, Pinot Blanc

Rosé: Most frequently made with Zweigelt

Red:

Zweigelt

St. Laurent

Blaufrankisch

Blauburgunder (Pinot Noir)

International varieties: Cabernet Sauvignon, Merlot and Syrah

Reds and whites from Trentino-Alto Adige and Friuli-Venezia Giulia in northeast Italy

Dry whites from Hungary

Reds and whites from France's Loire Valley

Late-harvest wines and Eiswein made from a wide variety of grapes, but primarily Welschriesling, Riesling and Scheurebe.

GREECE

Greek wine doesn't get a fair shake. Few civilizations can boast a winemaking history of over four thousand years. The Greeks were responsible for spreading vines throughout Europe, and an astonishing number of the wines we drink today are made from grapes descended from those vines. The wines form a natural pair with the country's cuisine, which features incredible meats and seafood, fresh produce and a sizeable assortment of aromatic herbs and spices. The flavors in these wines are, for the most part, quite accessible and enjoyable. Meanwhile, prices are reasonable and quality is on the rise.

So why isn't Greek wine more popular? The biggest obstacle to understanding Greek wine is getting familiar with the tongue-twisting grape names that confound even the most devout wine enthusiasts. Many ignore them completely rather than learn a new vocabulary of varieties that aren't grown anywhere else in the world. Complicating the matter further, English translations of grape names and growing regions often have confusing spelling variations. Nevertheless, the flavors of Greek wine and food are well worth exploring, and there's much more to

it than Santorini and gyros, so let's get started…

The first step is tackling those grape names. I'm sure there was a time for most of us when pronouncing "Cabernet Sauvignon" or "Sangiovese" seemed just as daunting as taking on these Greek varieties, so let's try a few. Agiorgitiko (Ah-yor-*yee*-tiko), Assyrtiko (Ah-*seer*-tiko), Moschofilero (Mos-co-*fee*-lay-ro) and Xinomavro (Ksee-*no*-ma-vro) are the four most important varieties grown in Greece, and the primary varieties covered below.

Next we have to make sense of Greece's major appellations. No straight line separates red wine regions from those specializing in whites. Wine is made throughout the country, but here we will focus on the quality regions most likely to export their wines to the American market.

Located among the Aegean Islands, about 120 miles southeast of the mainland, Santorini is exquisite, with bright white buildings hugging steep hillsides overlooking unimaginably blue water. The stunning beauty of this popular destination makes the complete enjoyment of the local beverage a foregone conclusion.

GREECE

Volcanic soils, dry, hot summers and strong winds create a unique climate for growing Assyrtiko, a white grape that's made into Greece's most recognizable and widely available wine. When handled properly it's fresh and vibrant, a perfect match for grilled seafood, and a delicious upgrade over innocuous Pinot Grigio or Sauvignon Blanc. Santorini is also the top source for Vinsanto, a barrel-aged dessert wine made from partially dried Assyrtiko grapes.

Peloponnese, which hangs by a thread onto the southernmost part of mainland Greece, contains several noteworthy regions. First is Nemea, the country's best appellation for the red grape Agiorgitiko, also known as St. George. Wines made from Agiorgitiko are typically medium-bodied, with an approachable fruit-forward style and soft acidity. The white grape Moschofilero is a specialty in Mantinia, where it is made into a wine that's reminiscent of a crisp, light-bodied version of Gewürztraminer because of its spicy quality and floral, rose petal aromas. In Patras, the Mavrodaphne grape is made into a fortified dessert wine of the same name. It is barrel aged, with flavors similar to tawny Port and Madeira.

Towards Greece's northern border lies the appellation of Naoussa in Macedonia. The red grape Xinomavro is king here, where it makes a high-acid wine (the name means "acid black"). It has aromas of red fruits, Mediterranean herbs and earthiness, and can age well.

Retsina, a white wine that derives its flavor from pine resin added to the grape must during fermentation, is made throughout Greece, though Attica in central Greece is the leading region for its production. Savatiano tends to be the grape of choice in this love-it-or-hate-it wine, which is at its best with an assortment of feta- and garlic-stuffed olives and other spicy *mezedes*, or tapas-like small bites.

We've just barely scratched the surface on Greek wine, but I assure you that you now have the necessary information to peruse the shelves of your favorite wine store in the pursuit of a diversified palate. *Yia mas!*

MAJOR WHITE GRAPES:

Assyrtiko

Moschofilero

Savatiano

MAJOR RED GRAPES:

Agiorgitiko / St. George

Xinomavro

Mavrodaphne

NOTEWORTHY SUB-REGIONS:

Santorini

Nemea

Naoussa

Mantinia

Patras

I offer two suggestions when preparing the Greek Burger: make it with lamb and pair it with the country's charismatic, rough-around-the-edges red wines, or make it with chicken and match it with various indigenous whites, particularly Greece's most famous wine, Santorini. The side dish puts a Greek spin on Campania's Caprese salad, with fresh mint, cucumber and super-tasty sautéed Haloumi cheese instead of basil, tomatoes and mozzarella.

RECOMMENDED COOKING METHOD: **Grill or cast iron pan**   YIELDS: **4 servings**

BURGER INGREDIENTS:

1 ¼ lbs ground lamb or chicken*

½ cup feta cheese crumbles

2 tbsp Greek seasoning blend (see below)

3 tbsp finely chopped mint

½ tsp salt

If preparing with chicken, add breadcrumbs as needed

GREEK SEASONING BLEND:

2 tsp dried oregano

2 tsp dried dill

2 tsp dried thyme

1 tsp ground coriander

1 tsp ground cinnamon

1 tsp salt

½ tsp ground cumin

½ tsp ground black pepper

½ tsp ground dried rosemary

ASSEMBLE WITH:

4 burger buns, split

Tomato slices

Feta cheese crumbles

Mint yogurt

MINT YOGURT:

1 tbsp olive oil

2 tbsp Greek seasoning blend

½ cup plain Greek yogurt

¼ cup fresh mint, finely chopped

GREEK-STYLE "CAPRESE" SALAD:

½ lb block Halloumi cheese, cut into 12 equal pieces

1 cucumber, sliced

¼ cup mint leaves, lightly chopped

2 tbsp olive oil, plus more for drizzling

Salt and pepper to taste

TO PREPARE

1. **Mix seasoning blend.**

2. **Combine burger ingredients** - Gently combine lamb or chicken with feta cheese, 2 tablespoons of the seasoning blend, mint and salt in a large bowl and mix gently. If preparing with chicken, add breadcrumbs as needed until the chicken no longer sticks to your hand. Form burgers and set aside.

3. **Prep salad ingredients.**

4. **Gather buns and toppings, set aside.**

COOK & SERVE

1. **Make mint yogurt** - Sauté 2 tablespoons seasoning blend in olive oil over medium heat for about 1 minute to cook the rawness out of the spices. Transfer to a small bowl and mix with Greek-style yogurt and mint. If you can't find Greek-style yogurt, drain ⅔ cup plain yogurt in a sieve lined with paper towels or cheesecloth for 10 minutes and wring out moisture.

2. **Heat grill to 400˚ for lamb.** For chicken, preheat a large cast iron pan on a 375° grill or on a stovetop burner set to medium-high heat. Drizzle the pan with vegetable oil just before adding burgers.

3. **Cook burgers 3 to 4 minutes per side, or until cooked to preferred doneness.**

4. **Assemble Greek-style "Caprese" salad** - While burgers are resting, heat olive oil in large sauté pan. Add Halloumi, and cook 45 to 60 seconds per side, or until lightly browned. Halloumi can also be grilled, but I've been happier with the results from sautéing. If you'd prefer to use the grill, rub each slice with olive oil on both sides prior to cooking. Arrange Halloumi, sliced cucumber and mint leaves on each person's plate. Drizzle with olive oil, and sprinkle with salt and freshly cracked black pepper.

5. **Serve, topping burgers with tomato, feta and mint yogurt.**

GREECE

Noteworthy appellations: *Grape(s):*

If preparing with chicken:

White: Santorini   Assyrtiko, Athiri, Aidani

         Mantinia   Moschofilero

         Retsina   Savatiano, others

         Various whites using Assyrtiko, Savatiano and Athiri, among others

If preparing with lamb:

Red: Nemea   Agiorgitiko / St. George

         Naoussa   Xinomavro

         Various reds made from Agiorgitiko, Xinomavro, Mavrodaphne as well as international
         varieties such as Cabernet Sauvignon

Whites from southern Italy: Insolia, Greco, Falanghina and Fiano
Reds from southern Italy: Aglianico, Negroamaro, Primitivo

Vinsanto, made from partially dried grapes, primarily Assyrtiko.

UNITED STATES

For many Americans, our introduction to wine was based on domestic bottlings. The labels are easier to understand than European labels, the flavors are easier to identify, grocery store shelves are heavily skewed towards California wines and there is an ocean of reliable juice at a decent price. But while experience is a good teacher, most wine drinkers will also find it useful to learn a bit about the rules and regulations governing American wine.

In 1978, the Bureau of Alcohol, Tobacco and Firearms (now the Alcohol and Tobacco Tax and Trade Bureau) created the American Viticultural Area (AVA) designation to identify a place of origin for grape growing. Identifiable, unique climatic conditions and geographic features that differentiate it from surrounding areas determine a viticultural area's boundaries. Prior to this, appellations were determined by political boundaries, such as state and county lines.

To use an AVA name (such as Rutherford or Knights Valley) 85% or more of the grapes used to make the wine must come from the indicated viticultural area. There are no limitations on which grape varieties may be used for winemaking within an AVA.

Fanciful proprietary names that don't disclose a grape or blend on the front label are common to many winegrowing areas throughout the United States. However, if a single grape variety is stated on a label it only needs to account for a minimum of 75% of the wine, so even varietally-labeled wines frequently blend in a complimentary grape or two. In Oregon, the minimum increases to 90%, and wine here is more likely to contain 100% of a variety than in California or Washington.

Ninety-five percent of a vintage-dated wine must come from the stated vintage if an AVA appears on the label. It drops to 85% when the label indicates an area as broad as a county or state, rather than an AVA.

The term "Estate Bottled" indicates that all of the wine was made from grapes grown in a vineyard that the winery owns or controls. These grapes must be from the same stated AVA as the winery, and the winery must crush, ferment, age and bottle the wine at their facility.

"Reserve" is found frequently on American wine labels, but has no enforced meaning. It implies a higher level of quality relative to a producer's other wines, but is no guarantee of overall quality.

CALIFORNIA'S CENTRAL COAST

In viticultural shorthand, the Central Coast of California is discussed as a unit, but in reality it's a vast territory, stretching 300 miles from end to end. The region has been fertile ground for innovation and quality over the past several decades, and at the center of it are the "Rhône Rangers" – winemakers who focus on warm-climate grapes indigenous to Châteauneuf-du-Pape, Hermitage, Condrieu and other appellations in France's Rhône Valley. Burgundy natives Chardonnay and Pinot Noir star throughout the cooler sub-regions, where nature provides all the necessary ingredients for the creation of wines with complex flavors, beautiful texture and fresh acidity.

Just south of San Francisco, at the very northern fringe of the Central Coast, the Santa Cruz Mountains AVA is responsible for some of the area's finest Cabernet-based wines. The combination of steep, high-elevation vineyards and a cool climate imbue the wines with the structure and balance that will allow them to evolve beautifully in the cellar for decades. Pinot Noir and Chardonnay are grown here with great success, along with some of California's most restrained expressions of Zinfandel.

Traveling south, Monterey County is most notable for its Pinot Noir and Chardonnay, particularly those grown in the Santa Lucia Highlands, Chalone and Monterey AVAs. But the temperature variations throughout the county allow for the cultivation of Cabernet, Merlot, Zinfandel and Rhône varietals as well.

Crossing from Monterey into San Luis Obispo County, your first destination is Paso Robles, the Central Coast's most well known viticultural area. Located in the rolling foothills of the Santa Lucia Mountains, the area is dotted with olive groves, oak trees and dry, scrubby grass. It's a laid-back, inviting town that has enthusiastically embraced its growing wine industry. While it's undeniably warm here, a number of distinct microclimates support the growth of a wide assortment of grapes. Cabernet and Merlot dominate in acreage, but much of this is located on Paso's relatively flat eastern side and is destined for big production wines. Most quality-oriented growers are located on the western side of town, where significant changes in elevation and climate equate to wines of varying styles, from reserved and structured to silky and voluptuous. The climate is an ideal match for those same Rhône varietals that thrive in the heat of Mediterranean France, led by Syrah and Grenache. Zinfandel flourishes here, where it's made into some of the state's most profound bottlings. Powerful Cabernet Sauvignon is also grown on the western side of Paso with excellent results.

At the tail end of San Luis Obispo lies the Edna Valley, a coastal shelf where the Pacific fog tempers the often brutal heat of inland California. Mild summers and warm fall months extend the growing season, allowing for complex flavor development in a mix of Burgundy and Rhône varietals. Pinot Noir and Chardonnay both perform very well here, but are sometimes trumped by stellar examples of Syrah, Grenache, Viognier and Rousanne.

Approaching the southernmost stop on the tour of the Central Coast, you notice the rolling landscape becoming increasingly green, intermixed with views of the Pacific, sprawling farmland or a quiet surf town. You're now in Santa Barbara County, where the Santa Ynez Mountains shift from running north-south to east-west. This unique geological pattern allows the breeze coming off the Pacific to drift through the area's vineyards unimpeded, making this one of California's coolest growing regions. Roughly ten miles from the Pacific, vibrant Chardonnay and Pinot Noir are grown in the Sta. Rita Hills and Santa Maria Valley AVAs. Progressing inland, the temperature rises with each passing mile, creating a twenty-degree difference between the area's warmest and coolest regions. As a result you'll see more of those heat-resilient Rhône varietals as you reach the eastern edge of the Santa Ynez Valley.

Your journey concludes in the city of Santa Barbara, where you can pop into several tasting rooms located a stone's throw from the pier. Enjoy a stroll on the beach and a feast of some fresh seafood for a perfect conclusion to your journey.

MAJOR WHITE GRAPES:

Chardonnay

Viognier

Roussanne

MAJOR RED GRAPES:

Syrah

Grenache

Pinot Noir

NOTEWORTHY SUB-REGIONS:

Santa Cruz Mountains

Monterey

Santa Lucia Highlands

Paso Robles

Edna Valley

Santa Barbara County

Sta. Rita Hills

Santa Ynez Valley

It doesn't get much better than this duck burger, which beautifully complements the immense range of wines in every shade of white and red made in this vast winegrowing area. The cheese comes from Monterey in the northern part of the Central Coast, while the pomegranates are from neighboring San Joaquin Valley. Thinly sliced baby cucumber adds a freshness that balances the flavors perfectly in one of the VinoBurger test kitchen's favorite recipes.

RECOMMENDED COOKING METHOD: *Cast iron pan*   YIELDS: *4 servings*

BURGER INGREDIENTS:

1 ½ lbs finely chopped duck (five duck breasts, fat and skin removed from three)

¼ cup finely chopped onion

2 tsp ground coriander seed

1 tsp salt

Breadcrumbs as needed

POMEGRANATE GLAZED ONIONS:

1 tbsp olive oil

½ medium white onion, thinly sliced

½ cup pomegranate juice

1 tbsp cider vinegar

ASSEMBLE WITH:

4 burger buns, split

Pomegranate glazed onions

Monterey Jack cheese slices

Mayonnaise

1 - 2 baby cucumbers, sliced lengthwise

SIDE DISH GRILLED TOMATILLOS WITH POMEGRANATE VINAIGRETTE:

4 large tomatillos, sliced ½-inch thick

Drizzle of olive oil

2 cups arugula

⅓ cup goat cheese crumbles

Salt and pepper to taste

POMEGRANATE VINAIGRETTE:

3 tbsp pomegranate juice

2 tbsp cider vinegar

2 tbsp olive oil

Salt to taste

TO PREPARE

1. **Combine burger ingredients** - Remove and discard layer of fat and skin from 3 of the 5 duck breasts. Cut all 5 breasts into 1-inch cubes, including the fat and skin on the remaining 2 breasts. In a food processor, grind duck to a coarse texture, with no large chunks remaining. Transfer to a large bowl and gently combine with onion, coriander, salt and breadcrumbs. Form burgers and set aside.

2. **Make pomegranate vinaigrette** - Whisk together pomegranate juice, cider vinegar and olive oil. Add salt to taste and set aside.

3. **Gather buns and toppings, set aside.**

COOK & SERVE

1. **Cook pomegranate-glazed onions** - Add onion and olive oil to a sauté pan over medium-high heat. Cook until lightly caramelized and add pomegranate juice and cider vinegar. Reduce heat to low and continue cooking until liquid has reduced to a light syrup.

2. **Preheat a large cast iron pan on a 375° grill or on a stovetop burner set to medium-high heat. Drizzle the pan with vegetable oil just before adding burgers.**

3. **Cook burgers 4 minutes per side, or until cooked to preferred doneness. Add Monterey Jack during final minute of cooking.**

4. **Grill or sauté tomatillos** - Drizzle sliced tomatillos with olive oil and grill briefly, about 45 seconds per side, until tomatillos are just barely tender and lightly browned. Remove and set aside.

5. **Assemble salad** - Toss arugula in 2 tablespoons of the pomegranate vinaigrette. Place a bed of arugula on each plate, topping with tomatillos and goat cheese. Dress with remaining vinaigrette, and sprinkle with a high quality finishing salt and freshly ground black pepper.

6. **Serve, topping burgers with baby cucumber slices, pomegranate-glazed onions and mayonnaise.**

TRADITIONAL PAIRINGS

Varietally-labeled wines:

White:
Chardonnay

Viognier

Roussanne

Marsanne

Rosé:
A small number of rosés are made from Rhône varieties

Red:
Syrah

Grenache

Pinot Noir

Cabernet Sauvignon

Zinfandel

Small amounts of several other French and Italian varieties

ALTERNATE PAIRINGS

Whites and reds from France's Rhône Valley

Syrah and Grenache from Australia

Provençal rosé

APPROPRIATE DESSERT WINE

Straw wine (vin de paille) using various white grapes

SONOMA

Bordered by the Pacific Ocean and separated from Napa Valley by the Mayacamas Mountains to the east, Sonoma County is a collection of thirteen appellations, with variances in climate and geography that allow for a wide range of grapes to thrive. The resulting wines are made in an assortment of styles that bring tremendous versatility to the dinner table.

Russian immigrants were the first to make wine here in the early 1800s, and by the 1820s Spanish Franciscan missionaries were rapidly increasing plantings throughout the valley. The area now boasts 65,000 acres of vineyard and over 250 wineries, from small family-run properties to ubiquitous grocery store brands pumping out hundreds of thousands of cases a year. The widespread availability and positioning of these brands frequently leads wine neophytes to believe that Sonoma and Napa produce vast quantities of wine. The reality is that the two regions combined produce just twelve to fifteen percent of the wine made annually in California, which of course is a tiny drop in the ocean of wine made worldwide.

A mere twenty miles separates Sonoma from Napa, but a mountain can make all the difference. In most of Sonoma's appellations, the influence of the Pacific Ocean creates ideal diurnal temperature variations and offers up cooling breezes throughout the day, allowing grapes to retain higher levels of acidity than those in Napa. This is why much of Sonoma County is planted to varieties that prefer cooler climates, principally Chardonnay and Pinot Noir. These grapes, when grown in the Russian River Valley and all points south, particularly Carneros (an appellation shared with Napa), can be made into stunning, nuanced wines with good acidic balance. Many Napa-based producers bottle Chardonnay and Pinot Noir, but the label is likely to reveal a Sonoma fruit source. The best of Sonoma can rival Burgundy in quality, though they are stylistically quite different. The Sonoma Coast is cool by California standards, but there is a telltale fruit-forward style to these wines. Chardonnay delivers layered richness when grown in the northern reaches of Sonoma, particularly in the rolling hills of the Alexander Valley, where the daytime temperatures can climb quite a bit higher than in those appellations closer to the ocean. This is more notably Cabernet country, where the grape achieves a ripeness that translates into a big wine with soft tannins and a silky texture.

SONOMA

Just west of the Alexander Valley you'll find the Dry Creek Valley and Rockpile viticultural areas, where Cabernet and Merlot are well represented, but Zinfandel takes center stage. Originally of Croatian descent, here it makes a wine packed with robust, spicy character. There's minimal tannin to extract from this thin-skinned grape, so the wine usually has a soft mouthfeel. The rich, peppery flavor of Zinfandel makes it an ideal pair with barbecue, burgers and other favorites off the grill, but tends to overwhelm lighter dishes. High alcohol content can be the Achilles heel of the finished wine, often stated at around sixteen percent...not a shy wine, by any means. But lower-alcohol, elegantly fashioned Zinfandel can be surprisingly Pinot Noir-like and food-friendly.

Chalk Hill and Knight's Valley are the warmest of Sonoma's appellations, and are the closest, both geographically and in style, to Napa Valley wines. Cabernet Sauvignon, Chardonnay and Sauvignon Blanc excel in these sub-regions. Syrah thrives here too, as it does throughout the valley. The challenge facing California Syrah is a lack of identity. American Syrah is its own breed, but consumers and wine professionals alike tend to lump it in with full-throttle Australian Shiraz. The best examples marry opulent blackberry and blueberry aromas with hints of Rhône-like meatiness, pepper and bacon.

Winemakers have been drawn to Sonoma for two centuries, including the aforementioned Russian immigrants and Franciscan missionaries, the "Father of California Wine" Agoston Haraszthy and several Italian families who have become some of the most recognizable names in the industry. With optimal grape varieties matched to each appellation, a wealth of talented winemakers and close proximity to one of the world's best enology programs at UC Davis, the future for Sonoma is shining bright.

MAJOR WHITE GRAPES:

Chardonnay

MAJOR RED GRAPES:

Pinot Noir

Zinfandel

Cabernet Sauvignon

Syrah

NOTEWORTHY SUB-REGIONS:

Russian River Valley

Carneros

Alexander Valley

Dry Creek Valley

Knights Valley

Part wine country cuisine, part California fusion, the Sonoma Burger combines the finest of local ingredients with flavors more commonly associated with Italian and Hispanic cuisine. Sonoma Valley's vinous past and present are closely knit with the two cultures; several of Sonoma's most well-known winemaking families came from Italy over a hundred years ago, and the Hispanic population has long been a driving force in making the valley what it is today. The mac and cheese side dish is a literal melting pot of the three cultures.

RECOMMENDED COOKING METHOD: *Grill*   YIELDS: *4 servings*

BURGER INGREDIENTS:

1 ¼ lbs ground turkey

¼ cup finely chopped shallot

¼ cup oil-packed, sun-dried tomatoes, chopped

1 tsp ground cumin

½ tsp salt

Breadcrumbs as needed, approximately ¼ cup

CILANTRO PESTO:

1 cup cilantro

¼ cup pine nuts

¼ cup Parmesan cheese

1 clove garlic

2 tbsp olive oil

¼ tsp salt

ASSEMBLE WITH:

4 burger buns, split

Cilantro pesto

Avocado slices

4 – 8 slices Pancetta (or bacon)

Pepper jack cheese slices

SIDE DISH MAC & CHEESE:

2 ½ cups small pasta shells or elbow macaroni

4 tbsp butter

4 tbsp flour

1 cup Chardonnay

1 cup half and half

½ cup grated pepper jack

½ cup grated queso fresco/quesadilla cheese

½ cup grated Parmesan cheese

½ tsp ground cumin

2 tsp finely chopped sage

1 tsp salt

Pepper to taste

TO PREPARE

1. **Make cilantro pesto** - Combine cilantro, pine nuts, Parmesan cheese, garlic and salt in a small food processor. Pulse, adding olive oil as needed to create a smooth texture.

2. **Prep mac and cheese** - Bring a large saucepan of salted water to a boil over high heat. Add pasta shells, and cook until al dente. Drain pasta and set aside.

3. **Combine burger ingredients** - Gently mix ground turkey, shallot, sun-dried tomatoes, cumin and salt in a large bowl. Add in breadcrumbs 1 tablespoon at a time until the turkey no longer sticks to your hand while mixing.

4. **Gather buns and toppings, set aside. Do not slice the avocado until after the burgers are cooked, as it will oxidize.**

COOK & SERVE

1. **Cook mac & cheese** - Place saucepan on burner set to medium-low heat and add wine. Reduce wine to about 1 tablespoon and add butter. Once butter has melted, add flour 1 tablespoon at a time, whisking constantly to avoid clumping. Once all flour is stirred in, add salt and cumin and cook an additional minute. Add in half and half and stir. Add cheese and stir until all cheese has melted. Add in cooked pasta and stir well to coat. Reduce heat to lowest setting. Stir in sage after the burgers are finished cooking.

2. **Heat grill to 400°.**

3. **Grill or sauté pancetta** - Cook 1 to 2 slices of pancetta per burger, depending on how thick or thin the pancetta is sliced. Cook until slightly crispy.

4. **Grill burgers 3 to 4 minutes per side, or until cooked to preferred doneness. Add pepper jack during final minute of cooking.**

5. **Slice avocado. Serve, topping burgers with pancetta, avocado and cilantro pesto.**

TRADITIONAL PAIRINGS

Varietally-labeled wines:

Sparkling: Several very good sparkling wines are produced in Sonoma, primarily from Chardonnay and Pinot Noir

White: Chardonnay

Sauvignon Blanc

Viognier

Rosé: Limited in production, but when available it may be made from any number of red grapes

Red: Pinot Noir

Zinfandel

Syrah

ALTERNATE PAIRINGS

Reds and whites from Burgundy, France

Primitivo from Puglia, Italy

Chardonnay, Pinot Noir and Zinfandel from California's Central Coast

---

APPROPRIATE DESSERT WINE

Icewine from Canada

NAPA

Winemaking in the Napa Valley began when George Yount first planted *vitis vinifera* in 1836. Charles Krug established the region's first winery in 1861, and in the next forty years would be joined by an additional 140 producers. However, few of these estates would survive to see the mid-1900s, as first the phylloxera louse devastated the valley's vines, then Prohibition crippled those who remained.

Today's Napa Valley thrives because of the dedication of those winemakers who brought the industry back from the brink. No one was more important to the development of modern winemaking in Napa than André Tchelistcheff. A Russian-born enologist, Tchelistcheff was studying in France when George de Latour of Beaulieu Vineyards hired him as winemaker in 1938. He had an immediate impact at BV, but more importantly he mentored newly-arrived visionaries, including Robert Mondavi, the most iconic figure in the history of the American wine industry. Tchelistcheff shared his extensive knowledge of fermentation techniques, had a gift for matching grape varieties to soil type, and preached the use of oak barrels in the fermentation and aging of wine.

By the early 1970s, world-class wines were being made in the Napa Valley. At the famous "Judgment of Paris" in 1976, a panel of mostly French wine experts conducted a blind tasting and shockingly crowned Stag's Leap Wine Cellars' Cabernet Sauvignon and Chateau Montelena's Chardonnay over the best from their native Bordeaux and Burgundy, the previously unquestioned leaders for the two grape varieties. Since then, the once-sleepy area has absolutely exploded. Over four hundred producers make wine in this thirty-mile stretch of vineyards. Many line Highway 29 and the Silverado Trail, which run parallel through Napa's core before converging in Calistoga. Familiar names and grand façades welcome thirsty travelers as they make their way up and down these two arteries and picturesque crossroads. A visit to any of these tasting rooms is likely to include a lineup of what Napa does best: Cabernet Sauvignon, Merlot and other Bordeaux-inspired red blends, as well as some excellent Sauvignon Blanc, Chardonnay and the occasional Syrah. The area is a beacon for anyone looking for top-flight wine combined with some of the country's finest dining and pampered relaxation. Though little wine is made within its boundaries, the quaint hamlet of Yountville is the center of it all, with small-town charm and restaurants that would make any food enthusiast swoon.

Along Highway 29, many of Napa's most recognizable wineries throw open their doors, waiting to pour a selection of their current vintages. Whites are made in a variety of styles, from bright, oak-free, citrusy Sauvignon Blanc to full-bodied, toasty Chardonnay and everywhere in between. The reds frequently feature ripe, dark fruit and sumptuous richness. While some wineries are guilty of offering more spectacle than substance, many deliver a drinking experience that serves as the "aha!" moment for numerous burgeoning oenophiles.

A stone's throw away you're on hallowed ground, where boutique producers are tucked into the hillsides of Rutherford, Stags Leap District and Oakville, offering scarce bottlings counted as some of the best wines in the world. St. Helena is the winemaking and cultural hub of the valley, and – I have to say it – home to one of the best burger joints I've ever been to, local legend Taylor's Refresher. Quiet side streets and folds of flowing vines protect farmer-operated micro-wineries from the glare of the spotlight.

Further off the beaten path, Calistoga, Angwin and Carneros offer idyllic wine country allure, where modest family-run estates dominate the scene. Mount Veeder, Diamond Mountain, Atlas Peak and Howell Mountain are downright remote, but offer intensely structured, age-worthy wines to those who make the journey. Beautiful Spring Mountain Road winds past prime hillside vineyards and darts through intermittent shafts of light breaking through the dense canopy of massive redwoods. Perched high atop the mountain with a glass in hand, looking down on the patchwork of vineyards below, you glow with contentment. Here is the good life, and you immediately understand why so many yearn to call this special place home.

MAJOR WHITE GRAPES:

Sauvignon Blanc

Chardonnay

MAJOR RED GRAPES:

Cabernet Sauvignon

Merlot

Syrah

Cabernet Franc

NOTEWORTHY SUB-REGIONS:

Rutherford

Oakville

Stags Leap District

Spring Mountain

Diamond Mountain

Howell Mountain

Calistoga

Carneros

Mount Veeder

The All-American combo of a burger and fries gets the VinoBurger twist! The Napa Burger is the lone recipe in this book that is inspired directly by a region's wines instead of its foods. The burger's seasoning is designed to replicate the aromas and flavors found in Napa's top red wines. Tarragon imparts a hint of licorice, while allspice and ground coffee mimic the effects of oak aging. To make the "reserve" version, try grilling the burger over hardwood charcoal with some oak chips to impart a sweet smokiness.

RECOMMENDED COOKING METHOD: *Grill*   YIELDS: *4 servings*

BURGER INGREDIENTS:

1 ½ lbs ground beef

¼ cup finely chopped shallot

1 tbsp chopped fresh tarragon

1 tsp ground allspice

1 tsp salt

BLACK PEPPER AND COFFEE CRUST:

2 tsp cracked black pepper

1 tbsp ground coffee

½ tsp salt

ASSEMBLE WITH:

4 sesame seed burger buns, split

Lettuce

White American cheese slices

Tomato slices

Mayonnaise

4 – 8 slices bacon

SIDE DISH NAPA FRIES:

1 ½ lbs russet potatoes

Peanut oil, for frying

1 tsp ground cardamom

2 tsp kosher salt

TO PREPARE

1. **Prep potatoes** - Cut potatoes to desired thickness for French fries. Immediately submerge cut potatoes in a large bowl of cold water with 2 tablespoons white wine vinegar. Soak 15 minutes, then drain and top with new water and vinegar.

2. **Combine burger ingredients** - Gently combine beef, shallot, tarragon, allspice and salt in a large bowl. Form burgers.

Mix together pepper, coffee and salt on a small plate. Roll each burger in the mixture to coat and set aside.

3. **Gather buns and toppings, set aside.**

COOK & SERVE

1. **Cook bacon** - Cook 1 to 2 slices per burger in large sauté pan.

2. **Blanch fries** - Fill a deep pot with about 4 inches or more of peanut oil, leaving at least 3 inches clearance from the top of the pot. Heat oil to 275˚. Drain potatoes and pat dry with paper towels. Add fries (in batches if necessary) to oil, and blanch until they just barely start to brown. Drain in a single layer on a baking rack. Fries will be limp, but cooked through. The cooking process isn't done, so leave the oil where it is, but turn the heat down to medium-low while cooking the burgers.

3. **Heat grill to 450˚.**

4. **Grill burgers 3 to 4 minutes per side, or until cooked to preferred doneness. Add American cheese during final 30 seconds of cooking.**

5. **Finish cooking fries** - While the burgers are resting, bring oil up to 375˚ and add fries. They will crisp up quickly, in about 90 seconds. Remove from oil and season with salt and cardamom immediately.

6. **Serve, topping burgers with lettuce, bacon, tomato and mayonnaise.**

NAPA

TRADITIONAL PAIRINGS

Varietally-labeled wines:

Red: Cabernet Sauvignon

Merlot

Syrah

Cabernet Franc

Petite Sirah

Zinfandel

Red blends, primarily made from Cabernet Sauvignon, Merlot and Cabernet Franc

---

ALTERNATE PAIRINGS

Reds from Bordeaux, France

South American reds

Reds from Bolgheri on Italy's Tuscan coast

APPROPRIATE DESSERT WINE

The majority of Napa's dessert wines are either late-harvest whites or Port-style reds.

OREGON

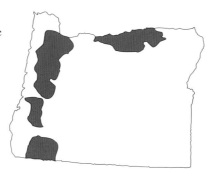

Oregon is a relative newcomer in terms of wine production. Grape plantings date back to the mid-1800s, but the area's true potential was unknown until the 1960s, when pioneering California winemakers headed north and concentrated on grape varieties from Alsace and Burgundy. Oregon is on roughly the same latitude as Bordeaux, France and Piedmont, Italy. Compare that to California's Napa Valley, which is on the same latitude as the southernmost part of mainland Italy, and it's easy to understand why Oregon's winemakers would specialize in cooler-climate grapes than their California counterparts.

The first plantings of *vinifera* grapes in the 1960s were centralized in the Umpqua and Willamette Valleys. Their surprising success plays a large role in Oregon's rapid ascent as a world-class growing region. It usually takes several decades, sometimes much longer, to find the varieties and clonal selections that create the perfect fusion with a region's climate and soil. However, these grape farmers got it right almost immediately, despite qualified minds telling them it couldn't be done here. If there were any doubts as to the quality of their wines, they were quelled in the 1980s following the success of Eyrie Vineyards' wine in two prestigious blind tastings of Pinot Noirs from around the world. Since then, the number of wineries and growers making wine here has increased tenfold.

Wine is made throughout Oregon, but the majority of producers are arranged along the western edge of the state, about fifty miles from the Pacific coast. The most important of these regions is the Willamette Valley and its six sub-appellations: McMinnville, Dundee Hills, Yamhill-Carlton, Eola-Amity Hills, Ribbon Ridge and Chehalem Mountains. Making wine here is not easy, but mountains to the east and west help to keep the valley sufficiently dry most years, while warm – but rarely hot – summers allow Pinot Noir to achieve ideal ripeness. The finished wines are capable of displaying a striking similarity to those of Burgundy. Finesse and balance are their key features; the wines aren't made to electrify the taste buds with a powerful melody of flavor, but rather to delight with gentle harmony. Pinot Noir, Riesling, Pinot Blanc and Pinot Gris from these AVAs represent the ultimate meeting ground between old world and new. The same could be said of the ethos of the community that produces them.

The Rogue and Applegate Valleys form the southernmost winegrowing area, bordering California. Syrah, Cabernet Sauvignon and Merlot are the grapes of choice here, not surprising given the success its southern neighbor has with these varieties. On the eastern border lies the Snake River Valley, an AVA shared with Idaho. This high-elevation area is quite dry, and with hot days and cool nights it offers a desirable climate for growing Riesling and Merlot, among others.

Three AVAs run along the state's northern border, all of which are shared with Washington. Very little of the largest AVA, the Columbia Valley, lies in Oregon, but its portion includes a variety of mesoclimates and changes in geography allowing for a wide selection of grapes to grow here, including Riesling, Chardonnay and a plethora of reds that thrive in the rain shadow of the Cascades.

Just as Argentina has Malbec and Australia has Shiraz, Oregon's identity is built primarily on the success of one grape. But those who look past Pinot Noir discover tremendous quality across an array of alternatives. There's a reason Pinot became – and will rightfully remain – Oregon's calling card, but sticking to the main roads is not what VinoBurger is all about. So, go ahead, pour the Pinot in a decanter and put it on the dinner table. But for education's sake, let's crack into something different while we cook.

MAJOR WHITE GRAPES:

Pinot Gris

Chardonnay

Pinot Blanc

Riesling

MAJOR RED GRAPES:

Pinot Noir

NOTEWORTHY SUB-REGIONS:

Willamette Valley

Rogue Valley

Umpqua Valley

Columbia Valley
(shared AVA with Washington)

Walla Walla Valley
(shared AVA with Washington)

OREGON

Oregon's identity in the wine world is based on its winegrowers' ability to craft beautiful representations of Pinot Noir, with elegance, balance and purity winning out over intense flavor. With that in mind, the recipe for the Oregon Burger uses a minimal number of ingredients, emphasizing the importance of the starting ingredients' quality. Use only the freshest wild-caught salmon and you'll have a burger that will sit comfortably at the dinner table alongside Oregon's finest bottles of Pinot Noir, Pinot Gris, Chardonnay or Pinot Blanc.

RECOMMENDED COOKING METHOD: *Non-stick sauté pan*   YIELDS: *4 servings*

BURGER INGREDIENTS:
1 ¼ lbs finely chopped fresh salmon, pin bones and skin removed
½ cup finely chopped leeks
2 tsp dried dill
1 ½ tsp salt
Breadcrumbs, only if necessary

LEMON DILL SAUCE:
3 tbsp sour cream
2 tbsp mayonnaise
1 tsp dried dill
Juice of ½ a lemon, about 1 tbsp

SAUTÉED FENNEL:
1 fennel bulb, thinly sliced
1 tbsp olive oil

ASSEMBLE WITH:
4 burger buns, split
Lemon dill sauce
Sautéed fennel

SIDE DISH RHUBARB SALAD WITH HONEY-LIME DRESSING:
1 cup rhubarb, sliced ½-inch thick
¼ medium red onion, thinly sliced
2 cups baby lettuce
¼ cup crumbled goat cheese
¼ honeydew melon, cut into bite-sized chunks
Salt and pepper to taste

HONEY LIME DRESSING:
2 tbsp olive oil
Juice of 2 limes
1 tbsp honey
Salt and pepper to taste

TO PREPARE

1. **Make honey lime dressing** - In a small bowl, whisk together olive oil, lime juice and honey. Add salt and pepper to taste.

2. **Make lemon dill sauce** - Combine sour cream, mayonnaise, dried dill and lemon juice in a small bowl and stir well.

3. **Combine burger ingredients** - Cut salmon into 1-inch chunks and place in a food processor. Pulse until no large chunks remain, but try to avoid grinding the salmon to a paste. Transfer salmon to a bowl and combine with leeks, dill and salt. Add breadcrumbs only as needed until salmon holds together, usually about 2 tablespoons. Form burgers and refrigerate until you are ready to cook.

4. **Gather buns and toppings, set aside.**

COOK & SERVE

1. **Sauté fennel** - In a medium sauté pan over medium-high heat, add olive oil and fennel. Sauté until fennel starts to brown lightly, and remove from heat.

2. **Assemble rhubarb salad** - Bring a small pot of water to a boil. Add rhubarb, and blanch for 1 minute. Remove rhubarb from water and immediately submerge in an ice bath for 2 minutes to stop the cooking. Drain and pat dry, then toss rhubarb with onion, lettuce and honeydew in a large bowl. Just before serving, toss with dressing. Serve, topping with goat cheese and a sprinkle of high quality finishing salt and freshly ground black pepper.

3. **In a large sauté pan with a tablespoon of olive oil, cook burgers over medium-high heat until golden brown, about two to three minutes per side or to preferred doneness. I like mine on the rare side, but for a more thoroughly cooked burger, place a lid on the sauté pan and cook an additional 3 minutes.**

4. **Serve, topping burgers with sautéed fennel and lemon dill sauce.**

OREGON

TRADITIONAL PAIRINGS

Varietally-labeled wines:

Sparkling: Several very good sparkling wines are made in Oregon using Chardonnay and Pinot Noir

White: Pinot Gris

Chardonnay

Pinot Blanc

Riesling

Gewürztraminer

Rosé: Little is distributed, but Pinot Noir is the grape of choice

Red: Pinot Noir

ALTERNATE PAIRINGS

Reds and Whites from Burgundy, France

Whites or Crémant (sparkling wine) from Alsace, France

Dry Riesling from Australia

APPROPRIATE DESSERT WINE

Icewine from Canada

WASHINGTON

There may not be a more exciting wine region in the United States to explore at this very moment than Washington State. The past two decades have seen its wine industry go from a budding region with a few standout producers to an area that has realized much of its potential. Quilceda Creek, Leonetti Cellars, Andrew Will and L'Ecole No. 41 – all wineries at the head of the class ten to twenty years ago – have been joined by Cayuse Vineyards and Charles Smith's K Vintners, among others, in crafting the state's most sought-after Bordeaux-inspired reds and stylish Syrahs. These wines can compete with the finest made anywhere else in the world. More important to the casual wine consumer is that quality across all price points is at its highest level yet. Thanks to affordable land and manageable operating costs, it is easy to find a thoroughly enjoyable, well-crafted bottle of wine from Washington, whatever your price range might be.

Washington's winegrowing regions focus primarily on French grape varieties, with Chardonnay leading all white plantings and Riesling running close behind. Cabernet Sauvignon and Merlot have been – and still are – the most planted red varieties, though

Syrah is gaining in acreage and holds out hope to become the state's most uniquely expressive wine.

In a state known for its cool and wet climate, almost all of the quality winemaking takes place in the Columbia Valley, in the desert-like rain shadow of the Cascade Mountains. The area receives a mere eight inches of rainfall annually; couple that with low-fertility soil which retains little water and irrigation becomes an absolute necessity. Warm days, cool nights and loads of sunshine help grapes to ripen evenly and develop complex flavors, while achieving fantastic balance and freshness.

The Columbia Valley growing region contains a number of smaller AVAs, each with its own personality. The Yakima Valley is the state's oldest AVA, and with over 12,000 acres planted to Chardonnay, Merlot and Cabernet Sauvignon, among other varieties, it represents one-third of all plantings in the state. Its neighbor to the south, Horse Heaven Hills, received AVA status in 2005, but its most highly regarded piece of land, Champoux Vineyard, put this region on the map over thirty years ago. The area features significant changes in elevation that allow for excellent hillside vineyard sites, while the moderating effect of the bordering Columbia River produces a constant cooling and drying wind similar to the Mistral in France's Rhône Valley. Straddling the Oregon border, the Walla Walla Valley contains just five percent of the state's vineyard acreage, but the quality of the wine produced here is undeniable. A handful of Washington's finest producers call Walla Walla home, and with a strong communal spirit it stands to reason that the top winemakers will help newcomers to achieve their best work. Smaller and lesser-known Rattlesnake Hills, Wahluke Slope, Lake Chelan, Snipes Mountain and Red Mountain all offer up a unique snapshot of Washington terroir.

Washington currently stands a distant second behind California as the United States' leading wine producer, with one tenth the vineyard acreage. A few large corporations pump out enormous amounts of clean, fruit-forward wines that offer good value, propelling Washington past the rest of the wine-producing states. But family wineries and growers still dominate the viticultural landscape, a trend that will hopefully hold up as we continue to see the number of world-class wines that emerge from the Pacific Northwest increase each year. Further experimentation with grape varieties and an ever-expanding understanding of the region's terroir will supply retailers and sommeliers with plenty of interesting wine to help consumers better understand why this corner of the world demands their attention.

MAJOR WHITE GRAPES:

Chardonnay

Riesling

MAJOR RED GRAPES:

Cabernet Sauvignon

Syrah

Merlot

NOTEWORTHY SUB-REGIONS:

Columbia Valley
(shared AVA with Oregon)

Walla Walla Valley
(shared AVA with Oregon)

Yakima Valley

Washington's great red wines shine when paired with this venison burger, which gets topped with some of the state's best produce: apples, pears and Walla Walla onions. The gaminess of the venison helps to bring out the complexities of Washington's awesome Syrah, Merlot and Cabernet. I couldn't possibly write a burger cookbook and not include onion rings, so here you have a side of golden, crispy, super-addictive Walla Walla onion rings.

RECOMMENDED COOKING METHOD: *Grill*   **YIELDS:** *4 servings*

BURGER INGREDIENTS:

1 ¼ lbs ground venison

½ cup peeled and finely chopped red apple

1 tsp salt

½ tsp ground black pepper

SAUTÉED PEAR & APPLE CHUTNEY:

1 tbsp butter

½ red apple, peeled and thinly sliced

½ green pear, peeled and thinly sliced

1 cup chicken stock

⅓ cup cider vinegar

¼ tsp salt

¼ tsp ground black pepper

ASSEMBLE WITH:

4 burger buns, split

Aged goat's cheese

Sautéed pear and apple chutney

Walla Walla onion slices (or other sweet onion)

Lettuce

SIDE DISH WALLA WALLA ONION RINGS:

2 Walla Walla onions (or other sweet onions), sliced into ¼-inch thick rings

1 cup milk

1 cup flour

⅓ cup cornstarch

1 tsp baking powder

1 tsp sugar

Salt

TO PREPARE

1. **Prepare onion rings** - Combine milk, flour, cornstarch, baking powder and sugar in a large bowl. Whisk until smooth. Fold onion rings into batter, being careful not to break the rings.

2. **Combine burger ingredients** - Gently mix venison, apple, salt and pepper in a large bowl. Form burgers and set aside.

3. **Gather buns and toppings, set aside.**

COOK & SERVE

1. **Make pear and apple chutney** - Melt butter in a sauté pan over medium heat and add apple and pear slices. Once apple and pear begin to brown, add chicken stock, cider vinegar, salt and pepper. Cook until all liquid has evaporated.

2. **Fry onion rings** - Fill a deep pot with about 4 inches or more of peanut oil, leaving at least 3 inches clearance from the top of the pot. Heat oil to 365°. Quickly but carefully, drop onion rings in one at a time. Work in batches if necessary to avoid overcrowding. Stir immediately to ensure that rings don't stick together. Remove when golden brown and season with salt.

3. **Heat grill to 400°.**

4. **Grill burgers 3 to 4 minutes per side, or until cooked to preferred doneness.**

5. **Serve, topping burgers with lettuce, onion slices, pear and apple chutney and goat cheese.**

WASHINGTON

TRADITIONAL PAIRINGS

Varietally-labeled wines:

Red:
    Cabernet Sauvignon

    Merlot

    Syrah

    Cabernet Franc

    Small amounts of Italian, Spanish and other French varieties

ALTERNATE PAIRINGS

Syrah from Chile

Cabernet Sauvignon and Syrah from California

Reds from Bordeaux or the Rhône Valley in France

APPROPRIATE DESSERT WINE

Late-harvest Riesling, Gewürztraminer and Semillon

Canadian icewine

Southern Hemisphere

ARGENTINA • CHILE • NEW ZEALAND • AUSTRALIA • SOUTH AFRICA

In ARGENTINA, the stated variety must account for 80% of the finished wine, as governed by the Instituto Nacional de Vitivinicultura. Few other laws have been created for Argentine wines, largely because the country is so new to the export market. Fine wine is a relatively recent development for Argentina, as it historically has produced bulk wines intended for domestic consumption.

In CHILE, the Ministerio de Agricultura and the Servicio Agricola y Ganadero combined with local wineries to create the country's wine laws and establish boundaries for its regions and appellations. A wine with a single variety listed on the label must be made with a minimum of 75% of said variety. At least 75% of the wine must come from the stated vintage, and 75% or more of the grapes must come from the stated appellation.

The NEW ZEALAND Food Safety Authority has established a few familiar rules that its producers must follow. Three-quarters of the grapes used in a wine must come from the stated appellation of origin. New Zealand wines intended for the American market must be composed of a minimum of 85% of the stated grape variety. When more than one grape is identified on a label, the grapes must be listed in order from the largest to the smallest percentage of the blend.

According to the rules created by the AUSTRALIAN Wine and Brandy Corporation, a wine that states a single grape on its label must be composed of 85% of the indicated variety. This is also the minimum percentage of grapes that must come from a stated appellation or vintage. As with New Zealand, a label that lists more than one variety must do so in order of the largest to the smallest portion of the blend.

In SOUTH AFRICA, the Wine of Origin (WO) designation indicates the source of a given wine. The stated grape must account for 85% of the blend, 85% of the wine must come from the stated vintage, but every last drop has to come from the indicated appellation. When more than one grape is listed, varieties must be labeled from largest to smallest percentage of the blend. An "estate" wine must be made from grapes grown, vinified and bottled on the estate's property, and must indicate an appellation of origin.

ARGENTINA

Mendoza is a strikingly attractive city, a metropolis with a very European vibe. The looming Andes serve as a reminder of its situation in the southern hemisphere, but the architecture and food culture are inspired reinventions of classic Spanish and Italian influences. The influx of immigrants that began in the 1870s and continued through the 1960s had a profound impact on the country's culinary identity. The same could be said of its winemaking, as Italian and Spanish immigrants brought their native grape varieties with them for cultivation in their new home. However, it's a transplant from another country that has found its way onto the dinner table of nearly every wine drinker looking for the most bang for their buck.

Malbec came to Argentina from southwestern France in the middle of the nineteenth century. While Malbec is best known in Bordeaux as a blending grape, it's in France's Cahors appellation where the grape originally took center stage. It still exists (and makes many exceptional wines) in its home nation, but most U.S. consumers today associate Malbec with the northwestern corner of Argentina. The grape's sensitivity to moisture-related vine maladies is not a hindrance in the desert-like conditions dominating the Argentine viticultural landscape.

Much of the quality wine in Argentina is made around Mendoza. Grapes are harvested from high-elevation sites in the foothills of the Andes, giving the finished wine intense color and flavor, soft tannins and great balance. Visitors owe it to themselves to spend a day or two on horseback in the pristine wilderness of the low Andes, a ridiculously beautiful and unspoiled land seen mostly by gauchos and free-range cattle. Cactus, scrub, baby goats and snow peaked mountains make overcoming vertigo and poor equestrian skills a worthwhile challenge.

As much as Malbec has done to put Argentine wine on the map, it's not the only grape that bears mentioning. Bonarda came to Argentina with Italian immigrants well over one hundred years ago, and makes wines of exceptional character in its "new" homeland. At least three sub-varieties of Bonarda exist in Italy; the version that crossed the ocean tends to produce black, smoky wines well suited to typical Argentine cuisine. A host of other red grapes are grown here, particularly Cabernet Sauvignon, Merlot, Tempranillo, Syrah and another Italian import, Sangiovese.

A fair amount of Chardonnay is grown in Argentina, but Torrontés makes for a far more exciting export. The varietal isn't new, just new to us. It has been farmed successfully for generations: today well over 30,000 acres are planted, primarily in the country's arid, cooler subzones. The best come from Cafayate, a high-elevation sub-region of Salta. There may be a relationship with a grape of the same name, native to the Ribeiro area of Galicia. Many immigrants from that corner of northwestern Spain settled in Argentina, but genetic tests linking the two grapes are at this point inconclusive. Regardless, the floral aromatics and stone fruit flavors found in a good Torrontés make it a wonderful aperitif wine, especially as a precursor to a glass of Malbec and a feast of Argentina's famously excellent beef.

Argentina's rise continues, with high-profile consultants from California and France helping local winemakers to push the envelope of possibility in this unique climatic and geographic situation. Others choose to bypass the consulting phase entirely and go straight to winery ownership, with premium vineyard real estate cheaper to buy and farm in Argentina than in second- and third-rate locales in their homelands. The sky is the limit, it seems, as the number of world-class wines emerging each year grows exponentially. It's remarkable to think of how prominent Argentina's wines will be if they can break through the one-grape-wonder category and prove there's more here than just Malbec. There's no reason to think they won't.

MAJOR WHITE GRAPES:

Torrontés

Chardonnay

Sauvignon Blanc

Chenin Blanc

MAJOR RED GRAPES:

Malbec

Cabernet Sauvignon

Merlot

Syrah

Bonarda

NOTEWORTHY SUB-REGIONS:

Mendoza

Salta

Patagonia

ARGENTINA

The Italian influence on Argentine cuisine is readily evident in the preparation of this burger, a favorite among the VinoBurger test kitchen participants. Grind your own Argentine grass-fed beef, and you'll certainly impress even the most discriminating gauchos. Chimichurri, the national condiment, infuses the Argentina Burger with parsley, oregano and garlic, and is also served on the side for dipping.

RECOMMENDED COOKING METHOD: *Grill*   YIELDS: *4 servings*

BURGER INGREDIENTS:

1 ¼ lbs ground beef

½ cup grated Parmesan cheese

2 tbsp finely chopped parsley

2 tsp fresh oregano

½ tsp paprika

½ tsp salt

CHIMICHURRI SAUCE:

½ cup olive oil

¼ cup Sherry vinegar

3 tbsp finely chopped parsley

2 tsp fresh oregano

1 clove minced garlic

Salt and pepper to taste

ASSEMBLE WITH:

4 burger buns, split

4 – 8 slices bacon

Provolone cheese slices

Tomato slices

Alfalfa sprouts

SIDE DISH HEARTS OF PALM AND TOMATO SALAD :

2 tomatoes cut into 4 slices each

14 oz can of hearts of palm, drained and cut in half

2 tbsp olive oil, plus more for sautéing

2 tsp Sherry vinegar

1 tsp salt

½ tsp ground black pepper

Parsley garnish (optional)

TO PREPARE

1. **Make chimichurri sauce** - Whisk together olive oil, Sherry vinegar, parsley, oregano, garlic and paprika. Add salt and pepper to taste. For best results, make this at least an hour ahead of time, up to a day in advance.

2. **Combine burger ingredients** - Gently mix beef, Parmesan cheese, parsley, oregano, paprika and salt in a large bowl. Form burgers and set aside.

3. **Gather buns and toppings, set aside.**

COOK & SERVE

1. **Cook bacon** - Cook 1 to 2 slices per burger in a large sauté pan. Discard drippings.

2. **Sauté hearts of palm; assemble salad** - Wipe sauté pan clean and set to medium-high heat. Add enough olive oil to lightly coat the surface of the pan. Sauté hearts of palm cut side down, about 1 minute or until they are lightly browned. Using a spatula, carefully remove hearts of palm from sauté pan. Assemble salad with tomato slices and hearts of palm, drizzling with olive oil and Sherry vinegar. Sprinkle with salt and freshly cracked black pepper.

3. **Heat grill to 400°.**

4. **Grill burgers 3 to 4 minutes per side, or until cooked to preferred doneness. Add Provolone during final minute of cooking.**

5. **Drizzle each bun with a small spoonful of chimichurri sauce. Top burgers with bacon, tomato and alfalfa sprouts. Serve with a side of chimichurri sauce for each person.**

ARGENTINA

Varietally-labeled wines:

Red:
Malbec

Cabernet Sauvignon

Merlot

Bonarda

Syrah

Sangiovese

Red blends made from the above grapes

Malbec from Cahors, France

Full-bodied reds from Chile

Everyday reds from Piedmont, Italy

Various late-harvest, typically made from white grapes

CHILE

Morning can be cold in the Casablanca Valley. Dirt roads stretch toward the Andes, lined as far as the eye can see by neatly ordered rows of vines. It's a good place to stretch the legs after long plane and car rides, as there is little danger of getting lost no matter how far one hikes from the winery or the main roads. In spring, the verdant land resembles some agricultural corner of northern Italy, with Sauvignon Blanc and Chardonnay growing especially well in the cool climate. The scale of farming is generally grand, and many wineries are of the brand-name variety, vast enough to supply chain stores across the U.S. and Europe.

Traveling south from Casablanca to Lolol in the Colchagua Valley is not a major distance, but a pit stop for a seafood-heavy lunch in the coastal city of San Antonio can make the journey seem leisurely. Chile's mountains exaggerate and isolate areas that would otherwise be neighbors; where Sauvignon Blanc and other cool-climate-loving grapes thrive in Chile's more northerly valleys, Cabernet Sauvignon and Carménère excel in the middle of the nation's vine-growing core. These varieties crave the heat that Rapel's Colchagua and Cachapoal Valleys offer. The latter grape is becoming a point of national pride. Since it was identified as distinct from similar-looking Merlot, Carménère has held out promise as this nation's version of Malbec, the grape that cemented bordering Argentina's reputation as a viticultural heavy-hitter. But the Andes between Chile and Argentina make all the difference. While Chilean Carménère may bear a faint resemblance to the elegant wines of St. Emilion in Bordeaux, Argentine Malbec can pack a wallop of tarry, spicy extravagance and concentration. Malbec in Argentina has developed into something wholly unique, while Chilean Carménère is, at present, largely imitative.

Still, Chile is emerging, finding identity across a wide range of grape types and mesoclimates. The dozen main growing regions all show promise, but remain difficult for outsiders to understand. The inscrutability of Chile's viticultural zones remains largely because these areas are (to varying degrees) still discovering or reinventing themselves. They are moving away from underperforming, dull grapes like Pais that blanketed the landscape for much of Chile's winemaking past. These valleys running inland from the Pacific defy easy classification, with each region yielding fruit of wildly varying quality. In general, the best fruit sources are those closest to the nation's capital of Santiago.

Broadly speaking, the nation is known for reds and whites made from French varietals: Carménère, Cabernet Sauvignon, Merlot and Sauvignon Blanc all hail from Bordeaux; Syrah, a Rhône varietal, is proving to have immense potential in several sub-regions of Chile; Chardonnay and Pinot Noir, both natives of Burgundy, do well in cooler valleys. It seems like every route forward is being tested. European wineries have poured money and experts into Chile in an attempt to grab a piece of this frontier. Land is relatively cheap, as is vineyard labor, leaving much room for growth in the coming years.

The diverse selection of wines in Chile provides ample pairing opportunities for the country's varied cuisine. Immigrants came to Chile from all over Europe and Latin America, putting their fingerprints on the country's food culture, which combines fantastic produce with poultry, beef, pork, lamb and, no big surprise, a lot of seafood. The Humboldt Current brings in copious mussels, scallops, abalone, crustaceans and other goodies to pair with Chile's refreshing whites, perhaps as an appetizer before diving into the Chile Burger and a bottle of red.

MAJOR WHITE GRAPES:

Chardonnay

Sauvignon Blanc

MAJOR RED GRAPES:

Carménère

Cabernet Sauvignon

Syrah

Merlot

NOTEWORTHY SUB-REGIONS:

Maipo

Colchagua

Maule

Casablanca

Aconcagua

Cachapoal

Curicó

CHILE

Modeled after empanadas de pino, the Chile Burger combines onion, black olives and raisins and gets topped with hard boiled egg, all authentic to this traditional Chilean recipe. I know, I know…the combination looks weird, but I assure you, it's tasty. A spiced cilantro mayo and Havarti cheese (unless you can find genuine Panquehue) finish it off. The "Tomatican-style" fritters are an adaptation of a traditional Chilean stew.

RECOMMENDED COOKING METHOD: *Grill*   YIELDS: *4 servings*

BURGER INGREDIENTS:

1 ½ lbs ground beef

⅓ cup raisins

½ cup pitted whole black olives

2 tsp dried oregano

1 tsp ground cumin

½ tsp paprika

½ tsp salt

AJÍ MAYONNAISE:

½ cup cilantro

⅓ cup mayonnaise

½ tsp chili powder

SAUTÉED ONIONS:

½ large onion, thinly sliced

1 tbsp olive oil

¼ tsp salt

ASSEMBLE WITH:

4 burger buns, split

Panquehue or Havarti cheese slices

Ají mayo

2 hard-boiled eggs, crumbled

Sautéed onion

SIDE DISH TOMATICAN-STYLE FRITTERS:

2 eggs, beaten

⅔ cup flour

1 cup corn kernels (drained/thawed if frozen)

½ cup diced onion

½ cup lima beans

2 tsp ground cumin

1 tsp salt, plus more for seasoning after cooking

SPICY TOMATO SALSA:

15 oz can diced tomatoes, well drained

1 small serrano chili, seeds removed

½ cup cilantro

Salt to taste

TO PREPARE

1. **Prep fritters** - Beat eggs in a large bowl. Add flour and stir well. Add corn, onion, lima beans, cumin and salt and stir.

2. **Make fresh tomato salsa** - Combine tomatoes with serrano chili and cilantro in a small food processor, and blend until smooth. Add salt to taste. Pour into a bowl and set aside.

3. **Make ají mayonnaise** - In the same food processor, pulse mayonnaise, cilantro and chili powder until well combined. Transfer to a bowl and set aside.

4. **Combine burger ingredients** - After rinsing the same food processor, purée raisins and black olives until smooth. Add to a large bowl with beef, oregano, cumin, paprika and salt and mix gently. Form burgers and set aside.

5. **Gather buns and toppings, set aside.**

COOK & SERVE

1. **Sauté onions** - Heat olive oil in a sauté pan over medium heat, and add onions. Cook until onions are completely soft and lightly caramelized. Add salt and stir.

2. **Fry fritters** - In a large sauté pan, heat ½-inch vegetable oil over medium-high heat. Gently add in fritter batter 1 heaping tablespoon at a time. Fry until golden brown, about 2 minutes per side. Sprinkle with salt after removing from oil and set aside.

3. **Heat grill to 400°.**

4. **Grill burgers 3 to 4 minutes per side, or until cooked to preferred doneness. Add Panquehue or Havarti during final minute of cooking.**

5. **Serve, topping burgers with sautéed onions, hard-boiled egg crumbles and ají mayonnaise. Top each fritter with a dollop of fresh tomato salsa.**

CHILE

TRADITIONAL PAIRINGS

Varietally-labeled wines:

Red:
Carménère

Cabernet Sauvignon

Syrah

Cabernet Franc

Red blends

ALTERNATE PAIRINGS

Reds from Bordeaux, France

Reds from Argentina

Reds from Washington

APPROPRIATE DESSERT WINE

Late-harvest whites, though Chilean dessert wines are a rarity

NEW ZEALAND

Grape vines have been planted in New Zealand for nearly two hundred years, but for all intents and purposes the country's wine industry is barely beyond its adolescence. Little noteworthy wine was made or exported prior to the 1980s, and it wasn't until the early part of that decade that any significant effort was made to enlighten the outside world to New Zealand's potential. Interest in winemaking was still on the upswing following the end of a temperance movement that lasted until the late 1960s. At the same time, an increase in international business travel exposed many New Zealanders to cultures with a greater appreciation for wine. As a result, vineyard acreage rapidly increased, with grape farmers transitioning away from underperforming, less fashionable varieties like Müller-Thurgau to more promising Sauvignon Blanc and Chardonnay. Critical acclaim in the early 1990s firmly established Sauvignon Blanc as the country's first variety of great distinction. It offered a singular flavor profile not expressed anywhere else in the world, and its intensely grassy aromas and vibrant acidity were an instant hit with many wine drinkers.

Located as far south as anyone dares to grow grapes, New Zealand is ideally suited to grape varieties that excel in a cool climate. They are best left relatively unadorned, so most white wines are fermented and aged in stainless steel, while light-bodied reds receive minimal barrel aging. This allows the fruit profile to shine through, as it's best to not cover up those delicate aromatics.

The southerly climate, paired with an almost omnipresent maritime influence, affords New Zealand's grapes an extended growing season, resulting in excellent flavor development and naturally high acidity. Excessive rainfall can be a concern, but massive mountain ranges offer some protection from the elements. In fact, these mountains can be so steep that they provide little opportunity for hillside plantings, so most of New Zealand's vineyards lay on flat or lightly sloping land. The country is divided into the North and South Islands, with wine regions spread fairly evenly across the two.

Sauvignon Blanc does well on both islands, but the most famous incarnation comes from Marlborough, located along the South Island's northern coast. Chardonnay is the second-most planted white grape behind Sauvignon Blanc, and here it is often made in the un-oaked or lightly-oaked style. It's the primary grape in Hawke's Bay, the country's second largest sub-region behind Marlborough. The two regions combined produce two-thirds of the country's wine annually. Soft, round Pinot Gris and brightly aromatic Riesling play smaller roles, but offer a great alternative to those who haven't been won over by New Zealand's assertive style of Sauvignon Blanc. The leader among red grapes, both qualitatively and in the number of planted acres, is Pinot Noir. It's at its best in Central Otago, the world's southernmost winegrowing region. High elevation and greater extremes between daytime and nighttime temperatures coax out the grape's nuance. Exceptional examples have earned their place in the discussion of the world's top sources for this finicky grape. Merlot and Cabernet run a rather distant second and third, respectively. These Bordeaux varieties tend to do best in the warmer sub-regions of the North Island, and receive more barrel aging than any other wines made in New Zealand.

New Zealand's cuisine is a blend of influences, from the traditions of the indigenous Maori, to those of the colonizing British and the incorporation of Asian flavors commonly found in Pacific Rim cuisine. Game birds and sweet potatoes were favorites of the Maori when they first arrived from Polynesia in the fourteenth century. Lamb may be New Zealand's best-known culinary export, but pork has also been popular since the British arrived with pigs in tow in the late 1700s. With so much coastline, mussels, rock lobster and other seafood naturally play a large role in New Zealand's cuisine, and are great pairs with the country's white wines.

MAJOR WHITE GRAPES:

Sauvignon Blanc

Chardonnay

Riesling

MAJOR RED GRAPES:

Pinot Noir

Merlot

NOTEWORTHY SUB-REGIONS:

Marlborough

Central Otago

Hawkes Bay

Martinborough

Nelson

Gisborne

You're probably expecting a lamb burger, but in order to pair with New Zealand's signature wine, Sauvignon Blanc, this recipe is made with pork. Mint kiwi salsa gives the New Zealand Burger a freshness that complements the zippy acidity of the country's white wines, while arugula has a peppery bite that cuts through the creaminess of the blue cheese. Sweet potato, or kumara as it's known in New Zealand, is a staple of the country's cuisine, so a side of freshly made sweet potato chips round out the meal.

RECOMMENDED COOKING METHOD: *Grill*   YIELDS: *4 servings*

BURGER INGREDIENTS:

1 ¼ lbs ground pork

2 celery stalks, finely diced

2 tbsp chopped mint

1 tsp ginger powder

1 tsp salt

KIWI MINT SALSA:

2 kiwis, peeled and diced

¼ cup chopped mint

¼ cup chopped shallot

¼ tsp salt

ASSEMBLE WITH:

4 burger buns, split

Blue cheese crumbles or Brie

Arugula

Kiwi mint salsa

SIDE DISH SWEET POTATO CHIPS:

1 ½ lbs sweet potatoes sliced into $^1/_{16}$-inch chips

Oil for frying

1 tsp salt

TO PREPARE

1. **Make kiwi mint salsa** - Combine kiwis in a small bowl with mint, shallot and salt.

2. **Combine burger ingredients** - Gently mix pork, celery, mint, ginger powder and salt in a large bowl. Form burgers and set aside.

3. **Prep sweet potato chips** - Place sweet potato slices in a bowl of water with 1 tablespoon of vinegar or lemon juice to prevent oxidation.

4. **Gather buns and toppings, set aside.**

COOK & SERVE

1. **Fry sweet potato chips** - In a deep pot, heat 3 to 4 inches of vegetable oil to 325˚. Be sure you have at least 3 inches of clearance from the top of the oil to the edge of the pot. Meanwhile, drain sweet potatoes and pat dry. Add chips to oil, working in batches if necessary to prevent overcrowding. Remove from oil when sweet potatoes are golden orange. Sweet potato chips will not be as crisp as regular potato chips. Sprinkle with salt immediately after removing from oil. Keep warm in an oven on its lowest setting.

2. **Heat grill to 400˚.**

3. **Grill burgers 3 to 4 minutes per side, or until cooked to preferred doneness.**

4. **Serve, topping burgers with arugula, blue cheese and kiwi mint salsa.**

NEW ZEALAND

TRADITIONAL PAIRINGS

Varietally-labeled wines:

Sparkling: A rarity, but a few are made using Chardonnay and Pinot Noir

White: Sauvignon Blanc

Chardonnay

Riesling

Pinot Gris

Gewürztraminer

Red: Pinot Noir

Merlot

ALTERNATE PAIRINGS

Sancerre or Pouilly-Fumé from the Loire Valley in France

Chablis from Burgundy in France

Pinot Noir from Oregon

APPROPRIATE DESSERT WINE

Mostly late-harvest, typically made from Riesling or Gewürztraminer.

AUSTRALIA

Production of fine wine in Australia is rooted in European heritage, as hard-working farmers from Germany, Poland and Switzerland poured their hearts and souls into tending the arid, infertile soil around Nuriootpa and other early winemaking centers. The techniques they espoused established Barossa as an epicenter of Australian winemaking; a remarkable land that these immigrants had been fortuitous enough to find and resolute enough to farm with a diligence derived from the *viticulteurs* of nineteenth-century Europe.

Today, the lure of easy money has brought change to much of Australia's wine industry. South Australia is a harsh place that will grudgingly yield a scant harvest of excellent fruit. But outside of the country's prime viticultural zones, land is abundant with enough water to irrigate. Grapes that originate in these fields have a fainter, less memorable sense of place to begin with, and adding copious water results in forgettable, bland wines. These are not bad wines, per se, and it's important to emphasize that their wild, exponential rise in popularity was not based solely on savvy marketing. The wines made from South Australia's less-exalted fruit sources are generally created by talented technicians; men and women who applied modern oenological innovations and streamlining to make the industry quite scalable. Without a doubt, Australia got ahead of the marketing curve, a foresight that allowed the industry to grow for decades at a pace that rattled many of the old winemaking nations. They devoured market share. A South Australian wine brand would offer consumers witty packaging, a name they could remember, and riper, cleaner, frankly more immediately enjoyable fruit than most plonk available from European co-ops and large-scale agribusiness at comparable prices.

However, low yields and dry farming are the hallmarks of great winemaking in Australia. Vines burrow deep to extract the innate character of this special land. Barossa's top vintners and their peers in nearby McLaren Vale, Padthaway and Clare Valley form the backbone of the country's quality wine production, where Shiraz reigns supreme. These deep, inky wines ooze with character, and are at once both muscular and silky. The Barossa Valley leads the pack in creating the archetype that many other Aussie reds try to imitate.

While Shiraz may be synonymous with Australia, other varieties thrive here as well. The aforementioned appellations are also a top source for bottles of Grenache that are close in complexity and age-worthiness to the dark, serious reds of Spain's Priorat, or the best from the Roussillon in France. To the south of Barossa lies the appellation of Coonawarra, where the combination of a cooler climate and the area's unique terra rossa soil offer Cabernet Sauvignon an ideal growing condition. The grape also does quite well in the similarly cool-ish Margaret River, far away on Australia's southwestern coast. Just south of Perth, this area is also home to several of the country's finest Chardonnays. Burgundian varieties Chardonnay and Pinot Noir co-mingle with a sampling of numerous red and white grapes in Victoria and New South Wales on the east coast. Small amounts of highly aromatic Viognier and Semillon verge on exotic when grown in the proper climates throughout southern Australia, while dry, vibrant and expressive Riesling from the Clare Valley remains a hidden gem. Dessert wines, or "stickies" as they're commonly called, can be world-class creations, packed with flavors ranging from honey and toasted nuts to molasses and caramel.

It's impossible to generalize the wines of an entire continent, but sadly that's what has happened as a reaction to the oversupply of uninspiring $7.99 Shiraz which has tarnished the entire country's reputation. This one-dimensional identity, unfairly ascribed to all Australian wine, has made it harder than ever to sell the good stuff. Successful branding has done much to grow the wealth of large-scale Aussie wine corporations, but it put downward price pressure on old-vine, low-yield, age-worthy wine from the country's top estates. Done right, Australia's reds can present as much unabashed hedonistic enjoyment as one can hope for out of a bottle of wine.

MAJOR WHITE GRAPES:

Chardonnay

Semillon

Viognier

Riesling

MAJOR RED GRAPES:

Shiraz

Grenache

Cabernet Sauvignon

NOTEWORTHY SUB-REGIONS:

Barossa Valley

McLaren Vale

Clare Valley

Coonawarra

Langhorne Creek

Padthaway

Margaret River

AUSTRALIA

The Australia Burger is a Barossa-centric spin on the national dish – the meat pie. The rules are pretty flexible as to what goes into one, and this recipe uses a mixture of lamb and beef seasoned with coriander and garlic. A splash of Worcestershire sauce is a tribute to the British who colonized Australia and brought with them the meat pie. Instead of topping the burger with ketchup, an ingredient that clashes with wine, I substitute a sun-dried tomato yogurt.

RECOMMENDED COOKING METHOD: *Grill*   YIELDS: *4 servings*

BURGER INGREDIENTS:

¾ lb ground beef

¾ lb ground lamb

1 tbsp Worcestershire sauce

1 clove minced garlic

2 tsp ground coriander

2 tsp fresh oregano, finely chopped

1 tsp salt

½ tsp ground black pepper

SUN-DRIED TOMATO YOGURT:

⅔ cup Greek-style plain yogurt

⅔ cup oil-packed, sun-dried tomatoes, finely chopped

1 tbsp tarragon, finely chopped

¼ tsp salt

1 tsp lemon juice

ASSEMBLE WITH:

4 burger buns, split

Onion slices

White cheddar cheese slices

Sun-dried tomato yogurt

SIDE DISH ZUCCHINI MASHED POTATOES:

1 lb russet potatoes

3 tbsp olive oil

1 medium zucchini, grated

½ cup half and half

1 cup grated cheddar cheese

½ tsp salt

2 tsp ground coriander

¼ tsp ground black pepper

TO PREPARE

1. **Make sun-dried tomato yogurt** - Combine yogurt, sun-dried tomatoes, tarragon, lemon juice and salt in a bowl and set aside.

2. **Combine burger ingredients** - Gently mix beef, lamb, Worcestershire sauce, garlic, coriander, oregano, salt and pepper in a large bowl. Form burgers and set aside.

3. **Gather buns and toppings, set aside.**

COOK & SERVE

1. **Make mashed potatoes** - Peel and cut potatoes into 1-inch cubes. Place potatoes in a large saucepan and fill with salted cold water. Bring to a boil over high heat.

While potatoes are cooking, grate zucchini and drain on paper towels to remove excess moisture. Sauté in olive oil until cooked through and lightly browned. Add coriander in the final minute of cooking.

When potatoes can be easily pierced with a knife (approximately 10 minutes), drain and return to stove, reducing heat to low. Mash lightly, and add in grated cheddar cheese, half and half, salt and pepper. Fold in sautéed zucchini. Set aside, reheating if necessary while burgers are resting after cooking.

2. **Heat grill to 400°.**

3. **Grill burgers 3 to 4 minutes per side, or until cooked to preferred doneness. Add Cheddar cheese during the final minute of cooking.**

4. **Serve, topping burgers with onion and sun-dried tomato yogurt.**

2005 Shiraz Barossa Valley
Seppeltsfield
Single Vineyard

firstdrop

FAT OF THE LAND

THE CREAM

750mL

AUSTRALIA

Varietally-labeled wines:

Red: Shiraz

Cabernet Sauvignon

Mourvèdre / Mataro

Merlot

Pinot Noir

Blends of the above grapes

Syrah and Grenache-based wines from the Rhône Valley and southern France

Most Spanish reds

California Syrah

Numerous sweet wines from Rutherglen, in Victoria, made primarily from Muscadelle and Muscat grapes. Also, *Botrytized* Semillon and Viognier from the Barossa Valley.

SOUTH AFRICA

The eager tourist finds much to photograph while traveling along the rural roads in the southern tip of Africa. It's hard not to stop and document every twist and turn, as day after day you believe you may never see another vista so beautiful. In spite of economic, political and cultural obstacles ahead and behind, the beauty of South Africa is readily apparent and it's easy to feel very happy to be in this unique place. Everything is so grand, raw, and in many instances, overwhelmingly majestic. But change is in the air in Cape Town. The wonderful vibrancy of the place is causing the world to rush in and threatens to wash away its distinct character. Fortunately, it will be hard to overwhelm the panorama of outsized mountains and sparkling ocean that are nearly omnipresent when traveling in the Western Cape.

South Africa's vinous origins go back to the seventeenth century, when vines were first planted in what is now Stellenbosch. By the early nineteenth century, South Africa was propelled to the forefront of the wine world when a dessert wine made by the estate Groot Constantia became a favorite of European royalty, including Napoleon. It's ironic that a country which produced one of the world's greatest wines more than three hundred years ago can be viewed as a New World upstart, still figuring itself out. South Africa's tumultuous past is well documented, and as its residents continue to focus on the future, so does its wine industry. The KWV, a winemaking co-operative formed in 1918, oppressed most aspects of South Africa's wine industry for over seventy years. Fiercely restrictive rules that limited the planting of new vines were finally eliminated in the early 1990s. With this newfound freedom, growers have the ability to explore new regions and to experiment with higher-quality plant materials, which in time will result in the proper match of vine to soil.

Much of South Africa's winemaking past, as well as its present, is tied to co-ops that pump out serviceable, but rarely noteworthy wines. However, greater interest in quality winemaking and outside investment is paving the way for a renaissance in the Cape's wine industry. Indeed, several producers are well on their way to reviving the country's standing among the wine cognoscenti to levels it enjoyed those centuries ago.

SOUTH AFRICA

On the western coast, the area surrounding Cape Town serves as the axis of quality-oriented winemaking, particularly in the rolling hillsides of Stellenbosch and Paarl. Pinotage – a genetic crossing of Pinot Noir and Cinsault – is a uniquely South African variety, and is among the country's most planted red grapes, along with Cabernet Sauvignon, Syrah/Shiraz and Merlot. South African reds tend to have a love-it-or-hate-it earthy, leathery funkiness, though better producers have limited or eliminated it entirely. Pinotage is especially likely to showcase this quality, but the best examples are far more fruit-driven. This light- to medium-bodied wine is a source of national pride, but it requires a makeover if there is any hope of making it into more than a local favorite. The most universally appealing Pinotage-based wines feature soft cherry fruit aromas and other attributes that liken it to its genetic parent, Pinot Noir. South Africa's white wines tend to offer greater purity of varietal expression, with Chenin Blanc, or Steen as it's known here, the country's most planted grape. Sauvignon Blanc and Chardonnay also excel, with the latter offering a surprisingly Burgundian quality in its finest examples.

The stunning mountains and the proximity to the South Atlantic Ocean create dramatic variations in the climate, which offers great opportunity for further growth and refinement of the country's signature wines. The move towards cleaner-tasting wines, crafted with greater control in the cellar, can only help to convert more enophiles into fans of South Africa's wines.

MAJOR WHITE GRAPES:

Steen (Chenin Blanc)

Sauvignon Blanc

Chardonnay

MAJOR RED GRAPES:

Pinotage

Cabernet Sauvignon

Syrah

Merlot

NOTEWORTHY SUB-REGIONS:

Stellenbosch

Paarl

Constantia

Robertson

While South Africa's red wines are coming on strong as of late, this burger is designed to go with the country's whites, particularly Chenin Blanc. The South Africa Burger combines many of the influences found throughout the country's varied cuisine. Chicken is mixed with Peppadew® peppers, a unique South African creation. The piquant spiciness of the peppers is balanced by the sweetness of mango chutney with a dash of curry powder. The burger gets topped with Gouda cheese, not surprising considering the early Dutch settlements in South Africa.

RECOMMENDED COOKING METHOD: **Cast iron pan**   YIELDS: **4 servings**

BURGER INGREDIENTS:

1 ½ lbs ground chicken

½ cup chopped Peppadew® peppers

1 tsp salt

Breadcrumbs as needed

MANGO CHUTNEY (FOR BURGER AND PARSNIPS):

2 mangos, peeled, cored and diced

⅓ cup white wine vinegar

½ tsp ginger powder

½ tsp curry powder

¼ tsp salt

ASSEMBLE WITH:

4 burger buns, split

Gouda cheese slices

Mango chutney

SIDE DISH CURRY ROASTED PARNSIPS WITH MANGO CHUTNEY:

1 ½ lbs parsnips, peeled

1 tbsp olive oil, or as needed to coat

1 tsp curry powder

1 tsp salt

TO PREPARE

1. **Prep parsnips** - Cut parsnips into even slices, approximately the same size as carrot sticks or thick-cut French fries.

2. **Combine burger ingredients** - Gently mix ground chicken, chopped Peppadews® and salt. Add breadcrumbs only as needed until burgers hold together. Form burgers and set aside.

3. **Gather buns and toppings, set aside.**

COOK & SERVE

1. **Roast parsnips** - Preheat oven to 350°. Toss parsnips in olive oil, curry powder and salt and spread out on a baking sheet. Roast 35 minutes, or until parsnips are tender and golden brown.

2. **Make mango chutney** - Add mango, white wine vinegar, ginger powder, curry powder and salt to a small saucepan and cook over low-medium heat until mangos are soft and liquid has reduced to a syrup. When finished, separate into two batches: one for topping burgers and one to serve with roasted parsnips.

3. **Preheat a large cast iron pan over a 375° grill or on a stovetop burner set to medium-high heat. Drizzle the pan with vegetable oil just before adding burgers.**

4. **Cook burgers 3 to 4 minutes per side, or until cooked to preferred doneness. Add Gouda during the final minute of cooking.**

5. **Serve, topping burgers with mango chutney.**

SOUTH AFRICA

Varietally-labeled wines:

White:
- Steen (Chenin Blanc)
- Chardonnay
- Sauvignon Blanc
- Gewürztraminer
- Semillon
- Viognier

Rosé:
- Made from Pinotage, Syrah, Cabernet Sauvignon and/or Cinsault

Red:
- Pinotage

Vouvray, Saumur, Savennières, or other Chenin Blanc-based white wines

Sauvignon Blanc from New Zealand, France's Loire Valley and California

Torrontés from Argentina

There are several options among sweet wines from South Africa, but one wine, Vin de Constance, was the pride of the country's wine industry in the eighteenth century. A modern-day version is relatively easy to locate at reputable wine retailers.

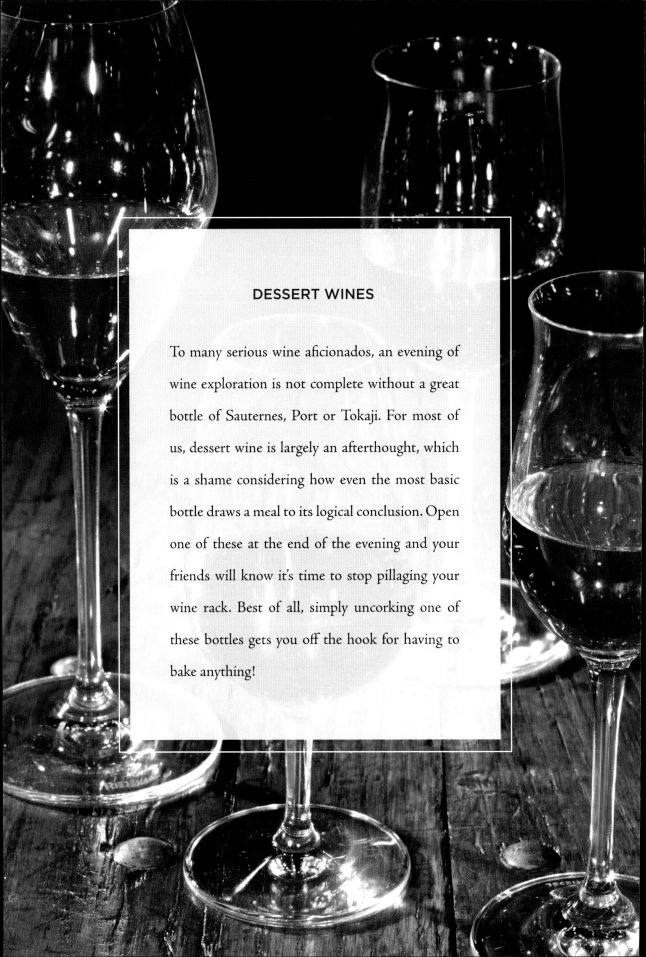

DESSERT WINES

To many serious wine aficionados, an evening of wine exploration is not complete without a great bottle of Sauternes, Port or Tokaji. For most of us, dessert wine is largely an afterthought, which is a shame considering how even the most basic bottle draws a meal to its logical conclusion. Open one of these at the end of the evening and your friends will know it's time to stop pillaging your wine rack. Best of all, simply uncorking one of these bottles gets you off the hook for having to bake anything!

Neutral grape spirit, usually in the form of brandy, is added to the fermenting grape juice during the winemaking process, which kills the yeast and halts the fermentation of any remaining sugar. Sweetness and alcohol content are determined by the amount of spirit added, and the point during fermentation at which it is added. A *vin doux naturel*, such as Muscat de Beaumes-de-Venise, is made by adding grape spirit to juice that has barely started fermentation.

At the other end of the spectrum are wines that receive a dose of sweet, concentrated grape juice after the wine has been fermented to dryness, such as sweet Sherries. The most popular fortified wine, Port, lies in the middle: grape spirit is added mid-way through the fermentation process, resulting in a wine of about 18-20% alcohol and moderate to pronounced levels of sweetness.

After fermentation and fortification, variances in aging will have the biggest impact on the finished wine's flavor.

* Sherry ages in a solera system; wine is transferred through a sequence of partially filled barrels over the course of many years. The air in the barrel oxidizes the wine, giving the wine nutty aromas and flavors. Because the solera system is an ongoing process where young and old wines are continually blended, Sherry is rarely vintage-dated. Instead, the year the solera was started may appear on the label.

* Tawny Port, which ages in barrel (frequently offered at intervals of 10-, 20-, 30- and 40-years in cask), becomes softer with age and takes on more caramel-like flavors.

* Bottle-aged Port (which may first spend a brief amount of time in barrel), including those that are vintage dated, hold onto their fruit profile. Inexpensive Ruby Port is grapey and approachable in its youth, while vintage Port has a darker fruit profile and is tannic, brooding stuff, requiring significant cellar aging.

* Late Bottled Vintage Port (abbreviated LBV) spends more time in barrel than vintage Port, but is intended to provide a similar drinking experience for less money. Quality is not as high, but the wine is drinkable far younger than vintage Port.

* Madeira is a fortified wine that came into being when it literally cooked during long voyages at sea, passing through the equator multiple times. The resulting wine became popular in the eighteenth century, and is now intentionally oxidized and cooked in a controlled environment. Casks are either set in a warm room over a period of several years, or subjected to the more modern, high tech *estufagem* process that cooks the wine over the course of several months. Madeira is reminiscent of tawny Port, but with higher acidity and a little more orange zest flavor. It ranges from fully dry to quite sweet.

- Marsala is made in a way similar to Sherry's solera system. Good Marsala shows hints of dried fruit, including apricots, dates and figs.

- Muscat-based *vin doux naturel* dessert wines, like those from Rivesaltes and Muscat de Beaumes-de-Venise, have flavors of apricots, orange blossoms and pineapples.

- Banyuls, a fortified Grenache from southern France, is produced in much the same way as barrel-aged Port and almost invariably displays notes of chocolate-covered cherries.

BEST EXAMPLES

Vintage and single quinta Port (Douro, Portugal)

Barrel-aged/tawny Port (Douro, Portugal)

Ruby Port and Late Bottled Vintage Port (Douro, Portugal)

Port-style wines from Australia and California

Madeira (Portugal)

Marsala (Sicily, Italy)

Sherry (Jerez, Spain)

Banyuls (Languedoc-Roussillon, France)

Muscat de Beaumes-de-Venise (Rhône Valley, France)

Rivesaltes (Languedoc-Roussillon, France)

Pineau des Charentes (Cognac, France)

AGING POTENTIAL: Tawny Port, Sherry, Madeira and Marsala have done most, if not all of their improving in barrel, so there is little incentive to age them further in the cellar. However, most will maintain the same level of quality for years.

Bottle-aged vintage Port and single quinta (single property) Port require at least ten years to enter their prime drinking window, if not significantly longer.

Better examples of *vin doux naturel* can age very gracefully, developing flavors of almonds, hazelnuts and plums.

SHELF LIFE ONCE OPENED: Vintage Port should be consumed in the same manner as a great dry red wine, meaning it is likely at its best consumed on day one, after the appropriate decant time. In most cases it should show well for two or three days, sometimes up to a week.

Tawny and Ruby Ports have a longer shelf life, lasting a month or more without issue.

Sherry's shelf life after opening ranges from a few days to a month. Lighter and drier Sherries show the effects of being open fairly quickly while richer, sweeter Sherries can last several weeks without noticeable deterioration.

Madeira is virtually indestructible. Since it has already been cooked and oxidized there is little you can do to harm it. Drink it over the course of several months.

Vin doux naturel is best consumed within a couple days of opening.

BOTRYTIS WINES

The top wines made from grapes affected by *Botrytis cinerea*, a fungus – more pleasantly referred to as "noble rot" – can be counted among the world's greatest wines, sweet or otherwise. When the conditions are right towards the end of the growing season, healthy, fully ripe grapes are exposed to moisture during the early morning hours, and begin to develop a rot that shrivels the grapes and concentrates the sugars. Warm, dry afternoons are required to stop the rot from developing too quickly and ruining the cluster. Following a highly selective harvest, the grapes are gently pressed and the super-concentrated juice is fermented into a wine of about 14% alcohol with noticeable sweetness. These wines have aromas and flavors of honey, tropical fruits, marmalade and orange blossoms, which turn nutty and caramelly with age. *Botrytis* wines are technically a subset of late-harvest wines (see pg. 242), but because of their elevated stature I present them on their own.

BEST EXAMPLES

Sauternes (Bordeaux, France)

Tokaji (Hungary)

Beerenauslese and Trockenbeerenauslese (Germany & Austria)

Ausbruch (Austria)

Sélection de Grains Nobles (Alsace, France)

Vouvray Moelleux and Doux (Loire, France)

Quarts de Chaume (Loire, France)

Various *botrytis* wines from Australia

AGING POTENTIAL: The best can last 50+ years. Great examples will last 20 years, though merely average examples should be consumed within five to ten years.

SHELF LIFE ONCE OPENED: Best consumed within a day or two.

LATE-HARVEST WINES

As the name suggests, late-harvest wines are those made from grapes that have been allowed to hang on the vine longer than those made into dry wines. During this extended hang time, sugar levels rise while acidity drops and skins become thinner, lowering the amount of tannin that may potentially be extracted during maceration. Most late-harvest wines will have moderate sweetness or more, and are made from both white and red grapes, though whites are more common. The most extreme example of late-harvest wine is Eiswein (icewine), made from grapes that are left to hang on the vine well into the winter. Frozen grapes are picked in the wee hours of the morning and crushed ever so gently, leaving the ice crystals mostly intact, releasing just the nectar of the grape. Making icewine is a risky endeavor, which is reflected in the pricing. Lesser-quality icewines are manufactured by placing grapes in commercial freezers. However, great icewines can stand shoulder-to-shoulder with the best of Sauternes and Tokaji.

BEST EXAMPLES

Eiswein/Icewine (Germany, Austria and Canada)

Numerous late-harvest wines from the United States, South America, Australia, New Zealand and more

AGING POTENTIAL: Lesser quality late-harvest wines are at their best in the first few years after release. The best are nearly immortal and will improve with additional time in the bottle.

SHELF LIFE ONCE OPENED: A week at most, but best consumed in the first two days.

DESSERT WINES MADE FROM PARTIALLY-DRIED GRAPES

Grapes are either hung or laid out on mats to dry partially, intensifying the flavor and concentrating the sugar content. The finished wine is quite full-bodied due to the reduced water content in the grape.

BEST EXAMPLES

Recioto (Veneto, Italy)

Vin Santo (Italy, particularly Tuscany; Greece)

Vin de Paille/Strohwein/Straw wine (Rhône Valley, France; Austria; Germany; Greece; California)

Pedro Ximénez Sherry, also fortified (Jerez, Spain)

AGING POTENTIAL: Like late-harvest wines, basic versions are at their best soon after release, but the best can age just as well as vintage Port, upwards of 75 years.

SHELF LIFE ONCE OPENED: Two to three days

SWEET SPARKLING AND *FRIZZANTE* (LIGHTLY SPARKLING) WINES

Brachetto, Moscato and Lambrusco are all fun Italian *frizzante* wines. The wines are naturally sweet as a result of an arrested fermentation, during which the temperature is brought down low enough to stop the yeast's conversion of sugar to alcohol, at which point the yeast is filtered out. With demi-sec (semi-dry) or doux (sweet) Champagne, the sweetness comes from the *dosage*, an addition of juice that all Champagne gets following *dégorgement*, the removal of sediment from the bottle. Demi-sec and doux Champagnes simply receive a sweeter *dosage* than normal brut Champagne.

BEST EXAMPLES

Moscato d'Asti (Piedmont, Italy)

Lambrusco (Emilia-Romagna, Italy)

Brachetto (Piedmont, Italy)

Demi-sec and doux Champagne (Champagne, France)

AGING POTENTIAL: Brachetto, Lambrusco and Moscato are best consumed as soon after release as possible. Demi-sec and doux Champagne may be aged far longer, depending on the pedigree of the producer and the quality of the vintage.

SHELF LIFE ONCE OPENED: As with any sparkling wine, the shelf life is very brief. Best consumed the same day it is opened.

DISTILLED GRAPE SPIRITS

Not wine, per se, but rather an end result of it, Grappa, Cognac and Armagnac are nevertheless an enjoyable way to finish a meal. Cognac and Armagnac are regions just north of Bordeaux in France, where wine is distilled into a spirit, which is then put in barrel to mellow out and soak up the influence of the wood. Grappa is distilled from the leftover skins, seeds and stems, collectively known as *pommace*. Grappa may or may not be cask aged.

BEST EXAMPLES

Grappa (Italy)   **Armagnac** (France)

Cognac (France)   **Pisco** (Chile)

AGING POTENTIAL: Does not improve after bottling.

SHELF LIFE ONCE OPENED: As with any other spirit, your only concerns are evaporation and thirsty houseguests.

Aromatized wines are flavored with various herbs and spices. Vermouth is by far the most widely known, which derives its flavor from spices and herbs such as cinnamon, nutmeg, coriander, cardamom, juniper, cloves and marjoram, among others. Barolo Chinato gets its flavor mainly from an infusion of rhubarb root and wormwood.

BEST EXAMPLES

Barolo Chinato (Piedmont, Italy)

Vermouth, also fortified (various, particularly Piedmont, Italy)

AGING POTENTIAL: Does not improve with age.

SHELF LIFE ONCE OPENED: Several weeks, but the sooner the better.

REFERENCES & FURTHER READING

The Oxford Companion to Food – Alan Davidson (Oxford University Press)

The Oxford Companion to Italian Food – Gillian Riley (Oxford University Press)

Culinaria France – Dominé / Beer / Feierabend / Schlagenhaufer / Ditter (H.F. Ullman)

Food and Wine of Greece: More Than 250 Classic and Modern Dishes from the Mainland and Islands – Diane Kochilas (St. Martin's Griffin)

The New Spanish Table – Anya Von Bremzen (Workman Publishing)

Regional Italian Cuisine – Reinhardt Hess & Sabine Sälzer (Barron's)

Cheese Primer – Steven Jenkins (Workman Publishing)

The All American Cheese and Wine Book: Pairings, Profiles & Recipes – Laura Werlin (Stewart, Tabori & Chang)

Herbs & Spices: The Cook's Reference – Jill Norman (DK Publishing)

The Wine Bible – Karen MacNeil (Workman Publishing Company, Inc.)

Vino Italiano; The Regional Wines of Italy – Joseph Bastianich & David Lynch (Clarkson Potter/Publishers)

Wines of the Pacific Northwest – Lisa Shara Hall (Mitchell Beazley/Octopus Publishing Group Limited)

The World Atlas Of Wine – Hugh Johnson & Jancis Robinson (Mitchell Beazley/Octopus Publishing Group Limited)

Jancis Robinson's Wine Course: A Guide To The World Of Wine – Jancis Robinson (BBC Books/BBC Worldwide Publishing)

www.erobertparker.com

www.winespectator.com

INDEX

Cilantro Coleslaw, 152–53, **154**

Cilantro Pesto, 184–85, **186**

Spicy Tomato Salsa, 216–17, **218**

Coffee

Black Pepper and Coffee Crust, 190–91, **192**

Corked wine, 20

Corn

Tomatican-Style Fritters, 216–17, **218**

Couscous

Chilled Couscous with Citrus Vinaigrette, 112–13, **114**

Cucumbers

Greek-Style "Caprese" Salad, 170–71, **172**

D

de Latour, George, 188

Denominação de Origem Controlada (DOC), 148

Denominación de Origen (DO), 116

Denominación de Origen Calificada (DOC/DOQ), 116

Denominazione di Origine Controllata (DOC), 78

Denominazione di Origine Controllata e Garantita (DOCG), 78

Dessert wines, 238

aromatized wines, 244–45

Botrytis wines, 241

distilled grape spirits, 244

fortified wines and vin doux naturel, 239–41

late-harvest wines, 242

from partially-dried grapes, 242–43

sparking and frizzante wines, 243–44

Dill

Lemon Dill Sauce, 196–97, **198**

Distilled grape spirits, 244

Dry wines, 18

Duck

Central Coast Burger, 178–81, **180**

internal cooking temperatures, 15

Languedoc-Roussillon Burger, 68–71, **70**

Penedès Burger, 144–47, **146**

Rosé Burger, 27–29, **32**

selection and preparation guidelines, 11, 13

E

Eggplant and Asparagus Banderillas, 132–33, **134**

Emilia-Romagna, 92–93

Emilia-Romagna Burger, 94–97, **96**

Epitrapezios Inos, 148

Estate Bottled wine, 174

Estate wine, 206

F

Fennel

Blanc de Blancs Burger, 26, 28–29, **30**

Sautéed Fennel, 196–97, **198**

Sicily Burger, 112–15, **114**

Feta cheese

Greek Burger, 170–73, **172**

Fish. *See also* Salmon; Tuna

internal cooking temperatures, 15

selection and preparation guidelines, 11, 13

Fortified wines and vin doux naturel, 239–41

France, 22

Alsace, 18, 36–37

Bordeaux, 48–49